CW01572649

Model Villages of the Nottinghamshire Coalfield

Chris Matthews
with Clare Hartwell

Model Villages of the Nottinghamshire Coalfield
by Chris Matthews with Clare Hartwell

Published in 2022
by Nottinghamshire County Council

Copyright © Chris Matthews, Clare Hartwell and Nottinghamshire County Council
ISBN: 978-1-7396780-0-5

Design by Chris Matthews
Printed by Hickling & Squires, Moorgreen, Nottinghamshire
Re-printed in 2023

CONTENTS

FOREWORD

Miner2Major is a Landscape Partnership scheme, supported by the National Lottery Heritage Fund, focusing on the natural and cultural heritage of the Sherwood Forest area. It is one of the aims of Miner-2Major to explore and celebrate the built heritage of its area. From the outset, an intention has been to investigate the old buildings of the Sherwood collieries, but on this occasion choosing not to focus on the industrial buildings of the pit heads, so few of which are now left, but instead to explore the colliery villages and how they were created. The thousands of houses that were built throughout Sherwood to attract the workers and their families from the end of the 19th century are an important legacy of the mining industry in Nottinghamshire. From the 1870s onwards these developments transformed the then rural villages and large landed estates of the Dukeries, creating new, vibrant communities that flourished on the shared values of hard work, cultural celebration and sport.

The lion's share of the work for this book and the short guides that accompany it, has been provided by Chris Matthews, with thanks also to Clare Hartwell the architectural historian and author who helped in defining the original scope of the project. Chris is a graphic designer, photographer and historian and is also the chair of the East Midlands Twentieth Century Society. He has perfectly succeeded in capturing the remarkable phase of Sherwood's history and beautifully presenting it in different formats.

We are very aware that this is not the whole story, we have for the most part, focussed on the Miner2Major partnership area. Although it cannot offer a complete account of mining villages in Nottinghamshire, we are pleased to have created a fantastic new resource. If you live in these villages or are visiting, we hope you will enjoy exploring their layout and plan forms. This beautifully illustrated book with its old photos and original drawings and the accompanying guides will help you in spotting the original features, details and arrangements of the streets. From the originators patriarchal intentions to the influence of contemporary urban planning concepts of the Garden City Movement, there is lots to explore and discover about the heritage of these colliery villages.

The Miner2Major Partnership Team

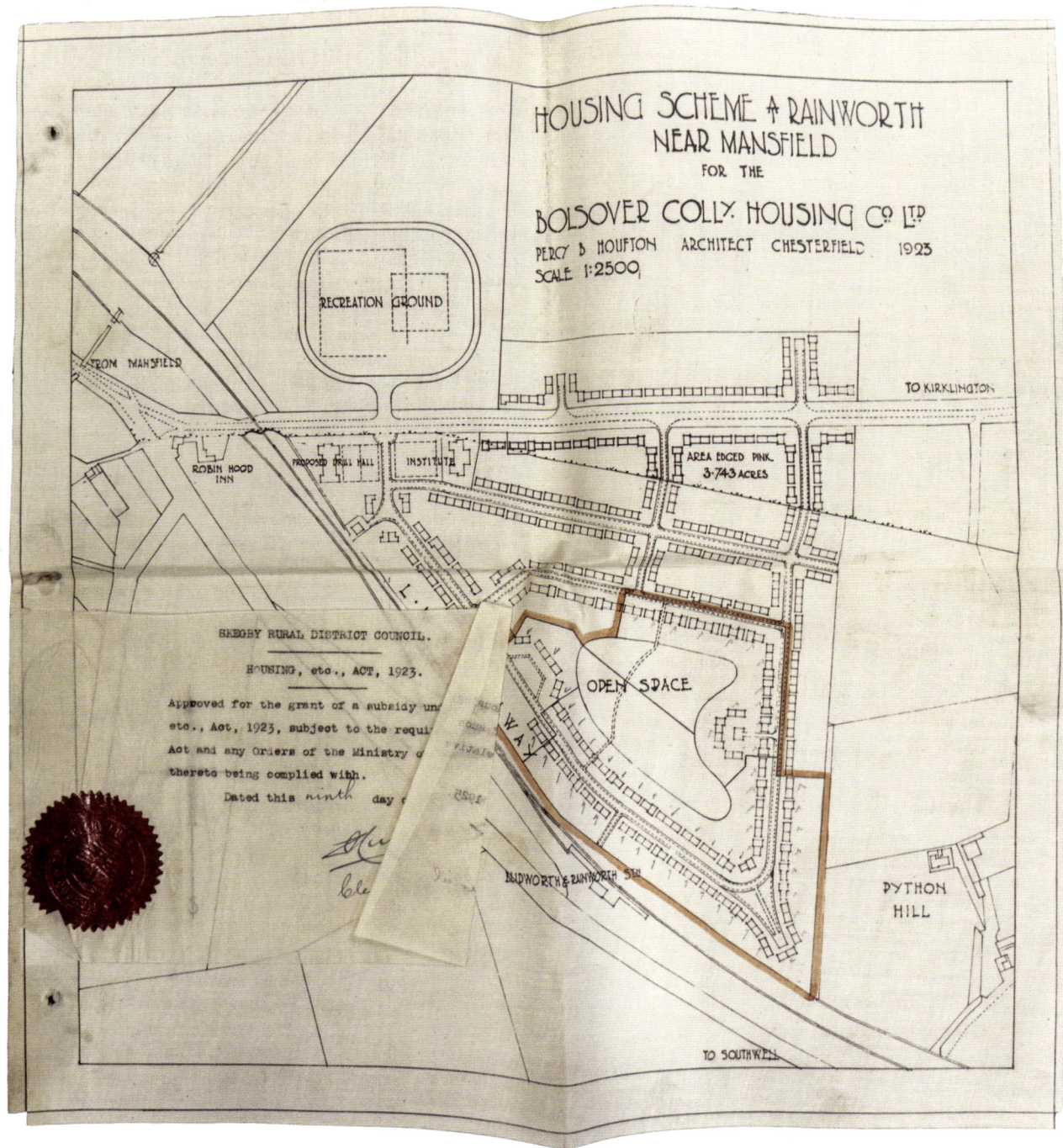

PREFACE
Researching the architecture of the Nottinghamshire coalfield

The plans and layout of the former mining villages in Nottinghamshire reveal not only their heritage but also a significant contribution to the national story. There have already been copious historical studies on the coal industry, both professional and amateur. Academic work has often been well funded and rewarded with high quality publications. The five volume *The History of the British Coal Industry* is a case in point.[1] Similarly work conducted at The University of Nottingham has brought many local insights, such as A. R. Griffin's *Mining in the East Midlands*,[2] and R. J. Waller's *The Dukeries Transformed*.[3] Recent work for Historic England and by Clare Hartwell has also provided fresh insight into the bricks and mortar of the Nottinghamshire coalfield.[4] Similarly there has been much work by David Amos and many local historians on the social and cultural nature of the Nottinghamshire coalfield.[5]

However, the architectural legacy of the Nottinghamshire coalfield poses a number of challenges, not least that its villages are recovering from the decline of the coal mining industry. As such, many buildings have been demolished; headstocks, offices, baths, institutes, churches and houses. Few buildings are protected by national listing, and some have been reconfigured for new purposes. A number of regeneration initiatives have helped to create new opportunities and the villages are now evolving into very different communities. Given these recent changes it can be challenging to interpret the historical legacy of the built environment. The architectural record is therefore incomplete, which is hardly surprising given that over 50 major collieries were developed in Nottinghamshire between 1860 and 1970.[6]

This particular study has focused on 12 model villages built by colliery companies in Nottinghamshire. The geographic scope has been set by the Miner2Major Landscape Partnership Scheme, which is managed by Nottinghamshire County Council and supported by the National Lottery Heritage Fund. It covers the model villages of the Dukeries coalfield, which were a huge development of the inter-war years. It also draws samples from the older villages of the Leen Valley and Mansfield districts. A full picture will therefore remain incomplete but it is hoped that this study will contribute towards a reappraisal, particularly the impressive string of colliery villages that were developed during the inter-war period. Clare Hartwell began the initial stages of research for six of the villages. Chris Matthews completed the research for those villages and undertook research for six more villages, critically appraised the research as a whole and gave the report its final editorial scope.

References

1. Of particular relevance, see: R. Church, *The History of the British Coal Industry Volume 3, 1830–1913: Victorian Pre-eminence* (Clarendon Press, 1986); B. Supple, *The History of the British Coal Industry, Volume 4, 1913–46: The Political Economy of Decline* (Clarendon Press, 1987); W. Ashworth, *The History of the British Coal Industry, 1946–1982, Volume 5: The Nationalised Industry* (Clarendon Press, 1986).

2. A. R. Griffin, *Mining in the East Midlands, 1550–1947* (Frank Cass, 1971).

3. R. J. Waller, *The Dukeries Transformed: The Social and Political Development of a Twentieth Century Coalfield* (Clarendon Press, 1983).

4. Arc Heritage, *The Heritage of the Nottinghamshire Coalfield: Historic England Project 6742* (2018); C. Hartwell, N. Pevsner, E, Williamson *The Buildings of England: Nottinghamshire* (Yale, 2020).

5. D. Amos & N. Barber, *Coal in the Blood: An East Midlands Coal Mining Anthology* (Trent Editions, 2021).

6. K. C. Edwards, *Nottingham & its Region* (British Association for the Advancement of Science, 1966), p.280

← Plans for Rainworth model village by the Bolsover Colliery Company. Submitted to Skegby District Rural Council, 1923.

--

Courtesy Inspire Nottinghamshire Archives DC/SW/4/8/23/4

Annesley Colliery and Village

1. INTRODUCTION:
Demand & Energy
Colliery Company Model Villages
of Nottinghamshire

← Annesley village, c.1930s. The conical tip in the distance was a hallmark of inter-war mining technology and has long since gone. Also notice that the houses have rear kitchen extensions by this point.
--
Courtesy © David Amos Collection

References

1. A. R. Griffin, *Mining in the East Midlands, 1550–1947* (Frank Cass, 1971), pp.62–65.

2. B. Supple, *The History of the British Coal Industry, Volume 4, 1913–46: The Political Economy of Decline* (Clarendon Press, 1987), pp.24, 183–184.

3. W. Ashworth, *The History of the British Coal Industry, 1946–1982, Volume 5: The Nationalised Industry* (Clarendon Press, 1986), p.435.

4. K. C. Edwards, *Nottingham & its Region* (British Association for the Advancement of Science, 1966), p.278.

Colliery Villages

Only traces of the Nottinghamshire coal-mining industry remain but what have survived are the colliery villages. Together they reflect the evolution of mining in the region and the ambition of the colliery companies who built them. Until the age of steam Nottinghamshire coal mines were generally a small addition to farming centered on the exposed (shallow) coalfield of the Erewash Valley.[1] To increase demand coal entrepreneurs successfully invested in a canal network, but their market went little further than the East Midlands. Their next initiative, which became The Midland Railway, created more rewarding possibilities by connecting the concealed (deep) coalfield to the lucrative London market. This was achieved in the second half of the nineteenth century, at first in the Leen Valley (Annesley, Bestwood, Newstead), and then later around Mansfield (Warsop, Welbeck, Rufford). This necessitated joint stock investment, improved technologies, more professional management and a larger workforce.

The colliery villages were crucial to this enterprise; their plan and form were designed to secure profits through paternalist means. The most impressive developments happened during the 1920s, when a string of huge mines were sunk under Sherwood Forest. These were technically advanced, professionally run and the villages were extensively built with suitable facilities. Blidworth, Bilsthorpe, Clipstone, Thoresby, and Ollerton represented the future of the industry and these places were considered a spectacular achievement.[2] Of course by then the national industry was in a state of decline; falling global demand coupled with the inefficiencies of the older coalfields were the root cause of increasing government intervention and eventual nationalisation. Over the course of the next forty years only three more collieries were sunk in Nottinghamshire (Calverton, Cotgrave and Bevercotes). Yet the great enterprises of the 1920s were justified: by the 1970s Nottinghamshire was arguably the most profitable coalfield area in the country,[3] while the East Midlands was the largest supplier of coal for electricity generation.[4]

In an era of modern energy production, dominated by quiet, often increasingly automated power generation it can be hard to imagine the impact and importance of the coal industry. Nottinghamshire played a significant role in this major industry until domestic coal production went into decline in the later part of the twentieth century. Today coal mining is condemned as environmentally unsustainable, but on grounds of conservation the colliery villages deserve reappraisal. The central ethos of these model villages also remains relevant: planned communities centered upon a demand for energy.

THE BRITISH COAL INDUSTRY
A Source of Wonder

For nearly 100 years until the Second World War, British coal was the most important traded form of energy in the world. It drove transport, electricity production, gas, manufacturing, steel making and domestic heating. Coal underpinned Britain's trade with the rest of the world: in short, coal was exchanged for food. By the 1920s nearly one million people were employed in the industry. The production and consumption of coal was an everyday occurrence of British life. The soot, smog and grime were an ugly problem of the industrial cities, but the sheer abundance of the coalfields were a source of prosperity and wonder.[5]

Competition & Efficiency

The harsh realities of falling global demand were keenly felt by the 1920s, particularly in what by then were the older and less productive coalfields, such as those in the North East. Colliery company amalgamation and government intervention were seen as increasingly necessary to improve efficiency in an age of declining exports and falling prices. The 1947 nationalisation of the colliery companies was both a technocratic solution to this same problem and a strong objective of mining unions who had deep rooted connections with the Labour government. In the meantime newer collieries such as those at Nottinghamshire were seen as exemplars of modernity; huge, efficient and highly productive.

Decline & Evolution

The strength of the coal industry was eroded as the global energy market became increasingly liberalised and competitive during the post-war period. The last Nottinghamshire coal mine (Thoresby) closed in 2015, one of the last deep mines to close in the UK and most of the industrial structures associated with mining have been demolished. However, what has survived are the colliery villages, particularly their housing, but also to a varying degree their amenities and memorials. Today these places are no longer centered on a single large employer and many people commute to neighboring towns and cities. The spoil tips and lagoons have been reclaimed while new housing estates grow around the edges.

↑ Clipstone Colliery, c.1939, showing the original headstocks before they were replaced in the 1950s.
--
From: *Bolsover Jubilee Souvenir, 1889–1939*, (Bolsover Colliery Company, 1939). Courtesy University of Nottingham Manuscripts and Special Collections, Oversize Em. O46 BOL

References

5 D. Edgerton, *The Rise & Fall of the British Nation: A Twentieth Century History* (Penguin, 2018), pp.80–87.

→ Bestwood Colliery, c.1940, the only buildings still recognisable today are the winding engine house and headstocks at the centre of the picture.
--
Courtesy © Picture Nottingham

↑ Boring at the coal face, Bestwood Colliery, c.1940.
--
Courtesy Inspire Picture Archive

THE NOTTINGHAMSHIRE COALFIELD
Pioneers: Leen Valley & Mansfield

The promises of the concealed coalfield in Nottinghamshire had been gradually realised from the 1860s, with developments along the Leen Valley at places like Annesley, Newstead and Bestwood. These pioneer colliery villages were initiated during a period of growing confidence in the British coal industry. Everything about these collieries was conducted on a large scale: the capital invested, depth of mine shafts, payroll, plant, output and villages. Not everything ran smoothly however; Annesley was undercapitalised and from 1875 there was a fall in British demand. Further development around Mansfield (Welbeck, Warsop Main and Rufford) had to wait until the turn of the century when the prospects of coal mining improved considerably.

Spectacular: The Dukeries & Sherwood Forest

The Nottinghamshire collieries that were developed during the inter-war period were spectacular in size, modernity, technology, workforce, housing, amenities and investment. On average, each shaft was 789 yards (721 meters) down and among the deepest in the country. Bilsthorpe, Blidworth, Clipstone, Thoresby and Ollerton gave the industry hope during a time of contraction due to changes in the global market. Their success was at odds with the inefficiencies of the older coalfields and these differences were often demonstrated during industrial disputes. Nottinghamshire miners became associated with breakaway unions and opposed to militancy, although this was largely due to the power and paternalism of the companies, rather than the working conditions.

← Thoresby Colliery, Edwinstowe, c.1939, showing Bolsover Colliery Company wagons beneath an impressive headstocks.
--
From: *Bolsover Jubilee Souvenir, 1889–1939*, (Bolsover Colliery Company, 1939). Courtesy University of Nottingham Manuscripts and Special Collections, Oversize Em. O46 BOL

↓ Rent agreement between Annesley Colliery and George Edwards, 1875. Here the tenant was required to keep the house clean and prohibited from keeping dogs, pigs or pigeons. A house inspector had the power to inspect every part of the house at any reasonable time. This is an example of how tied housing could impact upon the behaviour of miners.
--
Courtesy © David Amos Collection

Company Power

The character of these villages was determined by the colliery companies who carefully managed their huge investments. They leased the required land from the aristocracy and local elite, who earned royalties from each ton of coal that was extracted. These firms were expanding their extraction works and had originated from the older coalfields. Similarly the miners followed this pattern of migration. By the 1920s the most influential companies in the region were the corporate giants of the national coal trade. Staveley, Sheepbridge, Bolsover, Butterley, Stanton and Barber-Walker together changed the balance of mining activity in Britain. To contemporaries, this success was a result of advanced business methods and technological investment. To others the dependency of the workforce via tied housing represented the social threat of 'a new industrial feudalism'.[6]

MODEL VILLAGES
Paternal Capitalism

To attract the necessary manpower as much as a third of the initial expenditure of the colliery companies was on housing and the amenities necessary for village life. More than 6,000 houses were built in the twelve colliery villages investigated in this study, of which around 5,000 were constructed during the inter-war years. The approach of each colliery company varied, often depending on management style, architectural preference and nature of the

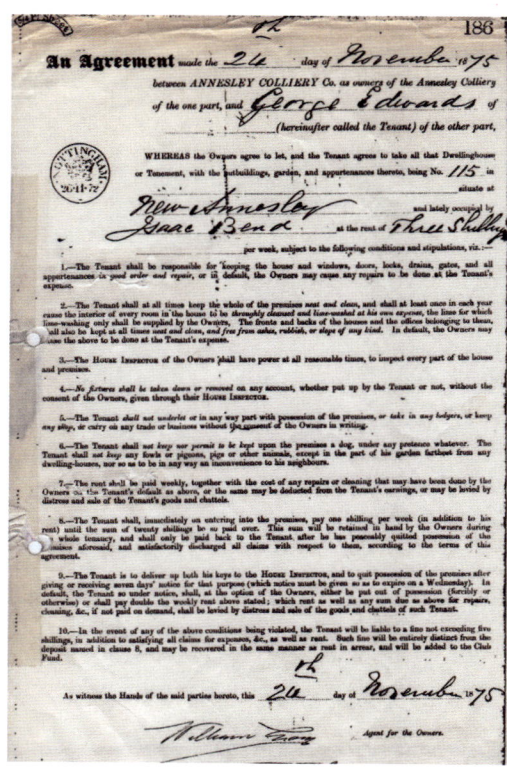

→ The Plough Inn, Ollerton. Pubs like these were built to accommodate social activities and provide temporary accommodation for mining contractors.
--
Courtesy Inspire Picture Archive

↑ Late nineteenth century terraces for miners at Bestwood Village. Bestwood is the most impressive of the late nineteenth century colliery villages in Nottinghamshire, notice the hipped dormers and slated canopies over the front doors.
--
Courtesy © Chris Matthews

References

6. B. Supple, *The History of the British Coal Industry, Volume 4, 1913–46: The Political Economy of Decline* (Clarendon Press, 1987), p.184.

7. Lord Robens, *Ten Year Stint*, (Cassell, 1972), pp.55–7.

location. The basic ethos was the same throughout; to control investment though paternalist means. Discipline, and therefore output, could easily be imposed on a workforce who stood to lose not only their job but also their house. The positive incentive for good behaviour was also strong: committed miners enjoyed the fruits of good housing, pay, social activities, opportunities for promotion and often the personal support of management. Colliery companies praised the virtues of 'fellow feeling'. They either supported or directly encouraged the provision of sports fields, village halls, welfare clubs, churches, shops, pubs, cinemas, surgeries and schools.

Coal dust made for thirsty work and pubs were almost a necessity. To encourage moderate behaviour their numbers were restricted, however those that were built were often large. This was to accommodate not only a considerable workforce but also social activities as well as temporary accommodation for mining contractors.

Fortunate Regulations

Compared to some of the other coalfields, Nottinghamshire was mostly developed at a later date and therefore under stricter building regulations, which resulted in higher standards of housing construction than would have happened in earlier years. Of the twelve colliery villages investigated in this study only New Annesley was built prior to the 1875 Public Health Act. Thereafter, individual privies and water supply were compulsory and streets offered a degree of spaciousness. Yet houses were cramped by later standards, often opened directly on to the road and most had to do without bathrooms. By the post-war period these Victorian terraces had to be modernised with new indoor toilets or kitchen extensions. In 1970 the miners' wives at Newstead Village confronted the Chair of the NCB Lord Robens to ensure that renovations were conducted according to their needs.[7]

← Cottage shops, Lyndhurst Avenue, Blidworth, by the Industrial Housing Association, 1920S. Housing designs from this period were more spacious than their Victorian predecessors.
--
From J. T. Walters, *The Building of Twelve Thousand Houses* (Ernest Benn, 1927). Courtesy University of Nottingham Manuscripts and Special Collections, Oversize Em. G15 WAL

The 1920s witnessed significant improvements in space standards and facilities following the Tudor Walters Report. Bathrooms and flushing toilets became essential, roads wider and density reduced. A variety of house types were recommended, which were often defined between having a parlour (best living room) and non-parlour.

Added to this, the 1920 Coal Act stipulated that miners' welfare institutes should be funded through the Miners' Welfare Fund. This was financed by an output levy on coal and administered by a committee of employers, royalty owners and trade unions.[8] The aim was to improve miners' recreation and social wellbeing with facilities for sport, dance, drama, music, reading and dining. From 1926 an additional levy was raised specifically to fund pithead baths, although the initial take up varied as some colliery houses were already provided with bathrooms. Unfortunately no pithead baths survive in any of the villages within this study. In 1952 the responsibility of Miners' Welfares was transferred to the Coal Industry Social Welfare Scheme (CISWO), which in 1995 became a charitable trust. Today CISWO secure the provision of recreational facilities (if needed) while management at the local level is undertaken by a charity specific to that area.

↑ The original 1920s entrance to the Newstead Miners' Welfare. To the right is the main hall and to the left is the lounge and games room.
--
Courtesy © Chris Matthews

The Industrial Housing Association

Not all colliery companies had the necessary capital to build on the scale required for modern mining. This problem was tackled by the Industrial Housing Association (IHA) which was established in 1922. It was a non-profit organisation initiated by a co-operative of colliery company directors and financed by government loans and grants. Essentially the IHA leased the housing estate to each colliery company it built for, who in turn managed the tenure. Nearly two thirds of the IHA villages in Britain were developed in the expanding coalfields of Yorkshire and the East Midlands. It was

References

8. W. Ashworth, *The History of the British Coal Industry, 1946–1982, Volume 5: The Nationalised Industry* (Clarendon Press, 1986), p.527.

→ Lord Aberconway, Chairman of Sheepbridge Coal & Iron Company, and Director of the Industrial Housing Association. Aberconway was considered an expert in his field and authored *The Basic Industries of Great Britain: Coal, Iron, Steel, Engineering, Ships. An Historic and Economic Survey* (1927).

--

From J. T. Walters, *The Building of Twelve Thousand Houses* (Ernest Benn, 1927). Courtesy University of Nottingham Manuscripts and Special Collections, Oversize Em. G15 WAL

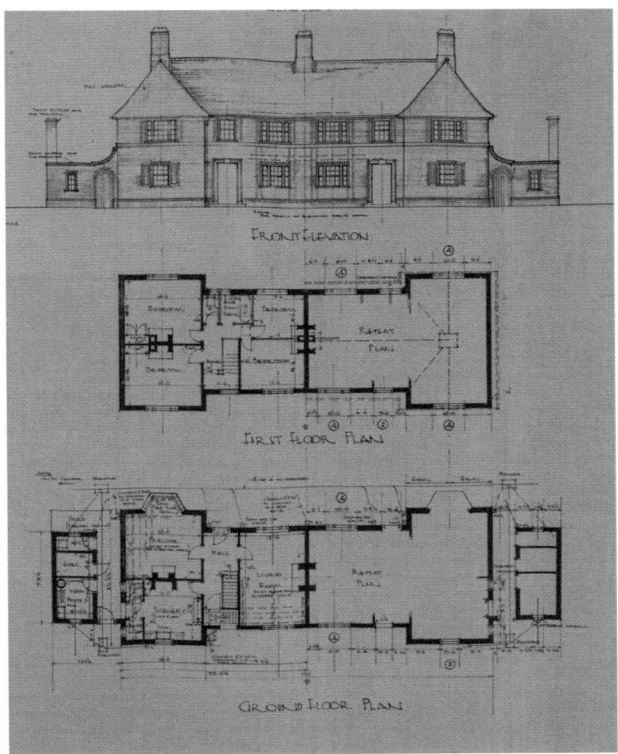

↑ Plan of houses intended for officials on Belle Vue Lane, Blidworth, designed by the Housing and Town Planning Trust on behalf of the Industrial Housing Association for the Newstead Colliery Company, 1925.

--

Courtesy Inspire Nottinghamshire Archives DC/SW/4/8/3/5

driven by industrialists who had a vested interest in this region, most notably Lord Aberconway and Arthur Markham of the Staveley and Sheepbridge colliery companies. They wasted little time in securing the services of perhaps the most respected figure in British housing at that time: Sir John Tudor Walters was given a directorship to oversee the design and building of the new model villages. The Tudor Walters Report was commissioned by the government in 1918 and set new national standards for housing in Britain. Walters was also president of The Housing and Town Planning Trust Ltd who were responsible for the architectural plans for the IHA.

Housing Management

The layout of each model village reflected the management structure of the colliery companies. Usually a large detached house was built or acquired for the colliery manager, often positioned separate from the housing estate but in view of the headstocks. Colliery managers were a consequence of the 1872 Coal Act and the professionalism required for overseeing huge mines. On the estate itself, the prime locations were reserved for under managers, clerks and engineers who were housed in large semi-detached housing nearest the pit entrance. The rest was designed for the miners themselves, but there were streets and houses that were more aspirational, which were usually larger and situated nearest the under managers. If the village was located close to the colliery then pithead baths were considered unnecessary providing houses were built with bathrooms positioned at a convenient distance from the ground floor entrance to the home.

← Late nineteenth century terraces at Newstead colliery village, showing rear yards with privies separate from the houses and a central alleyway. Although not brilliant, this was decent working class housing by Victorian standards, particularly when compared to urban slums or housing in the older coalfields.
--
Courtesy © Coal Authority, all rights reserved 2022

↓ Industrial Housing Association plans for Blidworth model village, showing how each house was provided with a living room, scullery, larder, bath and water closet (toilet). This was a significant improvement on nineteenth century housing facilities and space standards.
--
From J. T. Walters, *The Building of Twelve Thousand Houses* (Ernest Benn, 1927). Courtesy University of Nottingham Manuscripts and Special Collections, Oversize Em. G15 WAL

From Grid to Garden City

The nineteenth century colliery villages of the Leen Valley were planned along grids, linear routes and squares, a format common in Victorian England, and one which had its roots in Georgian rationalist development. Most of the houses were built using materials local to the area and in groups of basic terraces. Some colliery companies offered more spacious and decorated houses, but in most cases this approach tended to be reserved for officials and management. The villages around Mansfield developed at the turn of the century show the gradual change from the old Victorian grid, to the new garden city style that emerged in the twentieth century. However, compared to later developments these were sited in relatively suburban locations.

The new villages of the 1920s were far more remote from existing communities and as such their housing and amenities were more extensive. By this point colliery companies were committed to the designs of the arts and crafts, particularly for cottage style housing which was planned along geometric or picturesque layouts, similar to the way council housing was developed at the same time. They broadly followed the styles of the garden city movement, but not its ethos: these were villages dependent on mining and not self-contained. Industrial facilities and village amenities often undertook a greater variety of styles, such as neoclassical, beaux-arts, Romanesque, Gothic or neo-Tudor. By the 1940s there was a greater application of the modern movement, but this was mainly reserved for industrial plant. Colliery companies were committed to employing designers who could work according to their ethos. As such they employed architects of national and regional repute such as Thomas Worthington, A. E. Lambert, George Warner, Sir John Tudor Walters, Percy B. Houfton and Geoffrey Jellicoe.

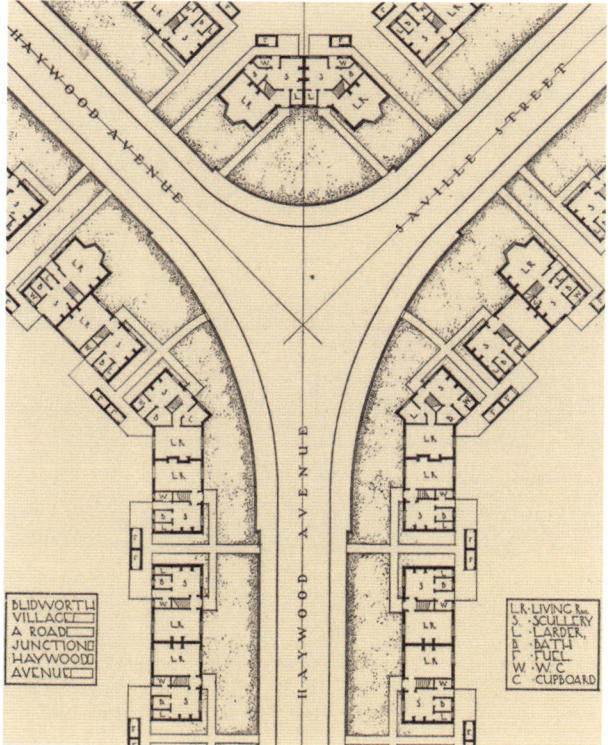

Following nationalisation the housing stock was handed over to the National Coal Board (NCB). The NCB were considered more distant and less paternal than their predecessors, but at the same time the miners were liberated from the social control of the old colliery companies. However, in terms of design the general suburban approach was the same as before. They followed local authority plans for housing estates and built their own housing stock quickly using prefabricated methods, such as the Cornish Type houses designed by A. E. Beresford & R. Tonkin. At the same time, district councils built housing on neighboring estates or gap sites, using garden city approaches to planning and brick building methods. The NCB also accompanied local authorities when it came to the government's Right to Buy policy of the early 1980s; houses were offered at a discount to existing tenants, which has since created estates of mixed tenure.

During the immediate post-war period the County Council had a backlog of schools and libraries to build in areas that were prone to mining subsidence. This problem was addressed by Donald Gibson, County Architect, who, alongside colleagues Dan Lacey and Henry Swain, developed a type of building that was resilient to movement and could be erected quickly. The essential component was a pin-jointed steel frame that could ride on a raft foundation with spring loaded cross bracing. Buildings were faced with flexible claddings such as hung tiles, weatherboard, aluminium and concrete panels. The system was marketed in 1957 with other authorities in mining areas as the Consortium of Local Authorities Special Programme (CLASP). A variety of models were developed by CLASP until 2006 when it became part of the Scape System Build Ltd. By this point 3,134 CLASP buildings had been built in the United Kingdom.[9]

Memorials

Mining was hard physical work, filthy and dangerous. Accident and death were a common occurrence, particularly when compared to many other occupations. The shared experience of these conditions engendered a very real sense of community and mutual support. Following the demise of the mining industry and closure of the collieries, many of the villages were decorated with mining memorials. Coal mining was a way of life for generations.

↓ Bilsthorpe Library, a modernist CLASP building by Nottinghamshire County Council, which was intended specifically for mining areas prone to subsidence.
--
Courtesy © Chris Matthews

→ Annesley pit wheel memorial and artwork. To the left in the distance stands Annesley colliery village.
--
Courtesy © Chris Matthews

References

9. E. Harwood, 'System Building', in *The Contemporary Journal 2* (March, 2020) see: https://thecontemporaryjournal.org/strands/critical-pedagogies/system-building

↑ Annesley village, c.1914, viewed from the hill to the south west. This image shows how the terraces were arranged in two rows, each split between 10 blocks of 8 houses. Notice how the terraces have no extensions to the rear, these were not developed until after the 1920s.

--

Courtesy © David Amos Collection

2. PIONEERS OF THE CONCEALED COALFIELD

The Leen Valley: 1860–1875
Annesley, Newstead, Bestwood

ANNESLEY
Clare Hartwell & Chris Matthews

Company & Village

In 1866 the British Association for the Advancement of Science met at Nottingham and was presented with a geological account of the sinking of Annesley Colliery.[1] Such was the interest concerning the pioneer collieries of the concealed coalfield, which began at Shireoaks in 1859. Along with High Park, Hucknall, Bulwell, Silverhill and Cinderhill, Annesley was among the earliest coal mines to be established in the Leen Valley district. Land owned by John Chaworth Musters of Annesley Hall was leased to William Worswick, who had coal mining interests in Leicestershire and formed the Annesley Coal Company. Shafts were sunk in 1865 and coal was reached in 1867.[2] The original housing and the building of the Victorian church illustrates collaboration between the land-owning family and colliery company in the creation of an industrial community.

Annesley colliery was the most challenging of the Leen Valley collieries, probably because it was undercapitalised and developed under a short lease – in 1904 it was brought out by the Hardwick Company from Holmewood, Derbyshire. In 1925 it was taken over by the New Hucknall Colliery Company and had to be substantially modernised.[3] The colliery remained in almost continuous production until closure in 2000. Pithead gear and associated buildings were demolished in 2008 and the colliery site has been developed for housing.

Housing

The settlement at Annesley retains miners' housing from the period of around 1870 consisting of two main types, basic terraces and semi-detached cottages. A settlement known as New Annesley was started after the pit had been established. Miners' housing was built in terraces of eight houses, in blocks of ten along two streets, giving 160 dwellings in all and erected between 1869 and 1873.

As these were built prior to the 1875 Public Health Act it is difficult to find out if each house was fitted with privy or water supply. Early

References

1. K. C. Edwards, *Nottingham & its Region* (British Association for the Advancement of Science, 1966), p.279.

2. David Amos, *A Brief History of Annesley Colliery 1865 – 2000* (2011, published online).

3. A. R. Griffin, *Mining in the East Midlands, 1550–1947* (Frank Cass, 1971), p.108–9.

← Annesley colliery sidings and village, 1932. On the hill to the left is the colliery manager's house and on the hill in the middle is All Saints' Church, and below that to the right is the mining village. This is a neat depiction of the economy and social structure. This photograph was taken by Hector Bowering, a colliery electrical engineer at the time.

--

Courtesy © David Amos Collection

Ordnance Survey maps suggest a degree of sharing between groups of four houses at an annex in the rear yard. By the later 1930s this arrangement was eradicated to make way for long gardens and ground floor extensions for sculleries which later became kitchens.[4] Indoor toilets and bathrooms were added by the NCB in the late 1960s. The terraces, originally known as Annesley Rows (also known as A Rows and Colliery Cottages) are ranged along streets now called Moseley Road and Byron Road. They are brick built and originally two-up, two-down, entered directly into the front room from the street, with a central staircase. It was customary to enter the house via the back door onto the yard while the parlour in the front was reserved for special occasions. Over time, the houses have since been faced with rough cast, pebble dashed dressing or render.

Management

At the top of the management hierarchy, the colliery manager resided at Eastview House, a detached house on a hill which overlooked the colliery. Below, on Newstead Road, are three pairs of semi-detached houses which were built for clerks and other officials.

A row of semi-detached houses was built along Derby Road at the behest of Caroline Chaworth Musters during the 1870s. The houses are at some distance from the terraces, along the main road. Known as The Grove or Annesley Grove, they are characteristic of model labourers' accommodation or estate workers' cottages of the period.[5] The semi-detached houses have front gardens and are built of rock-faced stone. They are executed in Gothic style, with pointed gables, prominent chimneys and mullioned windows*. The accommodation is superior to that of the terraces and census records suggest these houses were occupied by colliery management but not exclusively so. It was thought locally that they were estate houses for Annesley Hall.

↑ Semi-detached houses along Derby Road, built at the behest of Caroline Chaworth Musters during the 1870s. The spire of All Saints' Church is just visible on the right.

--

Courtesy © Chris Matthews

* mullioned windows
an aperture or window divided by vertical bars or piers usually of stone

References

4. Nottingham Insight Mapping, O/S Maps 1875–85, 1887–1899, 1912–1919 and 1937–40.

5. C. Hartwell, N. Pevsner, E, Williamson *The Buildings of England: Nottinghamshire* (Yale, 2020), p.98.

6. Nottingham and Southwell Diocese church history project: http://southwellchurches.history. nottingham.ac.uk/

The cottages are entered from the side, with two downstairs rooms and two bedrooms. Map evidence shows that there was an alley behind the houses and detached outbuildings, which were probably privies. By the end of the 1930s single-storey rear extensions of matching style and materials had been added, as shown on the 1938 OS map. The uniformity of design shows that the improvement was undertaken before the houses entered private ownership. Window joinery has largely been replaced. By 1938 a row of semi-detached brick and rendered houses had been built on Recreation Road close to the Byron Road and Moseley Road terraces. By this time considerable areas of housing had been built in the neighbourhood, but it is not certain which may have been built specifically for miners' families. Prefabs were also built at the rear of Recreation Road, following the Second World War and demolished during the early 1970s.

Amenities & Memorials

Between and behind the terraced houses there are areas of open space, where allotment gardens are marked on historic maps. A miners' welfare institute stood on Derby Road and has since been demolished. Apparently of inter-war date, it is shown on a map of 1938 beside a large sports ground. The former Post Office was built around the 1890s and still stands beside Annesley Cutting. A pair of winding wheels was erected near to the colliery site beside Newstead Road in 2009. In the cemetery there is a memorial to the men lost in the aftermath of a pit fire in 1877.

Other Buildings

A school (demolished) was co-funded by the Chaworth Musters family and the colliery firm. All Saints' Church was built to the designs of T. G. Jackson in 1874 to serve the village on land given by the Chaworth Musters family. Money was raised through local benefactors, fundraising events and local collections. It was substantially rebuilt by Robert Evans after a fire in 1907 destroyed the interior and roofs.[6] The building effectively replaced the small medieval church which (now ruinous) stands outside the village beside Annesley Hall. A cemetery beside the church had been completed in 1872 before work started on the building.

↓ The former Post Office beside Annesley Cutting. According to Ordnance Survey maps this was built sometime between 1885 and 1899.
--
Courtesy © Chris Matthews

← Park Road, Bestwood Village. Notice the quality of the brickwork on the end terrace gable, as well as the decorated lintels and string course along the front elevation. These houses were superior to the terraces at Annesley and Newstead.

--

Courtesy Inspire Picture Archive & Reg Baker

BESTWOOD

Clare Hartwell & Chris Matthews

Company & Village

Bestwood is a colliery settlement with a range of buildings erected for the Bestwood Coal and Iron Company (BCIC). It is the best designed village of its type in the Leen Valley area. The company was established by John Lancaster, an entrepreneur with coal mining interests in Lancashire, on land leased in 1872 from the 10th Duke of St Albans of Bestwood Lodge. BCIC was a successful enterprise that merged with Babbington Colliery Company in 1936 re-styling itself as B. A. Collieries Ltd.[1] The site remained operative until 1969, with coal diverted from Linby Colliery. Most of the industrial building and infrastructure was demolished, except the winding engine house, which was restored and opened as an attraction in 1995. The site was landscaped by the County Council.

Housing

Temporary housing was built in 1874 by the contractor J. E. Hall, for workers involved in sinking the shaft. The company started constructing housing almost immediately. The architect of these buildings and very probably additional housing dated 1876 was the noted Manchester practitioner Thomas Worthington.[2] The winding engine house was built to an Italianate design and may also have been designed by Worthington. It is almost certain that the Duke of St Albans influenced the design of the buildings, as at the nearby Bestwood pumping station, for which the lease of land was conditional on his approval of building designs. His interest in architecture is also illustrated by his choice of the architect S. S. Teulon, noted for his highly individual and inventive designs, for the rebuilding of Bestwood Lodge in 1862–5 and of the estate church, Emmanuel, erected in 1868–9.

↑ The colliery winding engine house and headstocks at Bestwood Village as they appear today. The winding engine house was built to an Italianate design.

--

Courtesy © Chris Matthews

References

1. In 1937 B. A. Collieries Ltd absorbed the Digby Colliery Company which owned Gedling Colliery. See: A. R. Griffin, *Mining in the East Midlands, 1550–1947* (Frank Cass, 1971), p.268.

2. C. Hartwell, N. Pevsner, E, Williamson *The Buildings of England: Nottinghamshire* (Yale, 2020), p.130.

3. Census Records, see: findmypast.co.uk

4. Historic OS mapping, local press reports.

* finial

a small decorative device to emphasize the apex of a dome, spire, tower, roof, or gable

↑ Detailed brickwork on miners' housing along Park Road, Bestwood. This plaque presents the date of construction as 1876.

--

Courtesy © Chris Matthews

↑ Additional housing built in the inter-war period on Church Road.

--

Courtesy Inspire Picture Archive & Reg Baker

The housing at Bestwood is an interesting example of relatively high-quality provision during the 1870s. The first phase went up on The Square and St Alban's Road. Foremens' houses stand at either end of a terrace of workers' housing. The foremens' houses are arranged in blocks of four houses with entrances in porches of two alternating designs, with tall gabled bays, prominent chimneys with stacks originally set diagonally and shallow bay windows. There is decorative and raised brickwork and a little timbering. The houses have back gardens and modern plans suggest that the porches open to a stair hall, with doors off to front and rear rooms. The terraced housing is simpler two-up two-down accommodation with small back yards and a narrow alley or entry between the rows at the rear. There is some decorative detail, such as characterful hipped dormers originally with finials* and slated canopies over the front doors. Plans suggest that a small stair hall was provided so that rooms were not entered directly from the street. The colliery managers resided in large detached houses at either The Sycamores (since demolished) on Moor Road or probably at the Edwardian Keepers House in Bestwood Park.[3] The Sycamores briefly became the HQ for the national Union of Democratic Mineworkers.

The second-phase terraces on Park Road of 1876 are also two-up two-down, but with both front and rear gardens. The nineteenth century Ordnance Survey maps show small buildings, probably privies, in the back gardens; most houses now have single-storey kitchen extensions. Modern plans suggest they have a separate staircase hall giving access to the two ground-floor rooms. Detailing includes plaques with the BCIC logo, shallow slated porches and some attractively decorative raised brickwork.

Additional housing was erected in the inter-war period, including semi-detached and terraced housing. The west and north sides of The Square were built up, as well as the south side of Park Road, north side of Church Road, the east side of St Alban's Road and new streets were also laid out. The housing harmonises with earlier work in terms of scale and materials, extending the grid pattern established with the earliest housing of the village. Additional building took place after the middle of the twentieth century.

Amenities

A recreation ground (now cricket pitch) and allotment gardens within The Square and off Park Road are shown on nineteenth-century OS maps. Bestwood Village Social Club, at the west end of Park Road became a miners' welfare and community centre; it was built as a village hall in 1928. At its centre is a large arts and crafts brick building with a pitched roof. It was later surrounded by modern flat roofed extensions. The Bestwood Hotel on Park Road was built in 1896 and is marked 'Institute' on early twentieth century OS maps.[4] The building is a good example of late Victorian architecture by an unknown architect. It probably had its origins as a working mens' club or miners' institute, for which fundraising events were being held in the 1880s.

← The church of St Mark, School Walk, Bestwood Village. Built in 1887 and designed by J. Medland Taylor. The light and airy interior was originally heated by glazed brick fireplaces, in both the nave and trancepts.
--
Courtesy © Chris Matthews

Other buildings

The former colliery office building (the Clock Tower) was executed in Italianate style with a tower, to designs by Thomas Worthington.[5] The use of brick with stone dressings creates a polychromatic effect and reflects Worthington's interest in Continental Gothic styles and the influence of John Ruskin. The plans were approved in 1873.

The church of St Mark was established as a mission church and built in 1887 to designs by the Manchester architect J. Medland Taylor. The land was donated by the Duke of St Albans and the colliery company, each paid £600 towards the costs.[6] The building is a good example of a modest church by this architect with an exposed timber roof, stained glass of some quality and furnishings with local associations.

The Lenton School Board became concerned about the need for a school in Bestwood, because of a growing population in an area distant from existing schools. The exception was an establishment referred to as a 'dame school' capable of taking fewer than thirty children. Such establishments were private institutions, often with a poor educational reputation. This stood to the south of the east end of Park Road. Eventually land was acquired from the Duke on the other side of the village and plans solicited from the architect to the colliery company, though the identity of the architect at this time has not been established. After the Bestwood School Board was started as a separate entity, the school opened under its auspices in May 1879. It was designed in the arts and crafts style with some decoration below the eaves and may originally have had a gothic south facing window.

↑ Bestwood Coal and Iron Company offices. The building was designed by Thomas Worthington in 1873.
--
Courtesy © Bestwood Winding Engine House Project (2013-2015)

References

5. C. Hartwell, N. Pevsner, E, Williamson *The Buildings of England: Nottinghamshire* (Yale, 2020), p.130.

6. Nottingham and Southwell Diocese church history project: http://southwellchurches.history.nottingham.ac.uk/

→ Newstead village, c.1970, showing the original late nineteenth century terraces in the foreground with the colliery headstocks to the rear.
--
Courtesy © Coal Authority, all rights reserved 2022

↓ Newstead village mortuary chapel, Hucknall Road, built 1875.
--
Courtesy © Chris Matthews

NEWSTEAD VILLAGE
Chris Matthews

Company & Village

The Newstead Colliery Company commenced work in 1874 on land leased from the estate of William Frederick Webb of Newstead Abbey. Webb was a respected member of the local gentry and a big game hunter. Newstead colliery village is one of the oldest of its type in the concealed coalfield of Nottinghamshire, and the last of the original Leen Valley collieries to be developed prior to a fall in demand for coal which lasted until the 1890s.[1] Its Victorian terraces are contemporary with those at Annesley and Bestwood. Newstead shares similar characteristics with these places, but its layout is less formal. The Newstead Colliery Company was a joint venture by two firms originating from the Chesterfield area of North East Derbyshire; Staveley Coal and Iron Company, and the Sheepbridge Coal and & Iron Company.[2] Staveley would later develop Warsop Main Colliery, where the similarities with Newstead are marked; linear groups of Victorian terraces accompany inter-war estates built by the Industrial Housing Association (IHA). In the 1920s Newstead Colliery Company also developed Blidworth, again employing the resources of the IHA but on a much bigger scale. This was testament to the success of the Staveley–Sheepbridge group, which on the eve of nationalisation had the greatest output of any colliery undertaking in the country.[3] At Newstead the original colliery houses have always been known as the Old Village and the 1920's development as the New Village.

References

1. A. R. Griffin, *Mining in the East Midlands, 1550–1947* (Frank Cass, 1971), p.105.

2. Durham Mining Museum Website, www.dmm.org.uk

3. A. R. Griffin, *Mining in the East Midlands, 1550–1947* (Frank Cass, 1971), p.163.

← Tilford Road, Newstead. Terraces built by the Newstead Colliery Company for miners, sometime between 1875 and 1885.
--
Courtesy © Chris Matthews

↓ Parlour type houses for under managers and clerks on Hucknall Road. Built during the early 1920s by the Industrial Housing Association.
--
Courtesy © Chris Matthews

Housing & Amenities: The Nineteenth Century

By the 1880s the Newstead Colliery Company had built 170 houses which ran along a grid between what is now Tilford Road and Chapel Terrace.[4] These post-date the 1875 Public Health Act and therefore were built with individual privies and water supplies. Incorporated in these terraces were corner shops, a post office and an old farmhouse. The earliest maps show allotment gardens north and south of Tilford Road and Chapel Terrace, a cricket ground along Hucknall Road and football field beside Station Road.[5] Housing for the management was located nearest to the colliery on the eastern side of the Midland Railway line. After nationalisation these houses became part of the main industrial complex and were demolished following the closure of the mine in 1987. Further provisions from outside organisations were developed by the close of the nineteenth century; a station hotel, cemetery chapel,[6] a Primitive Methodist chapel (demolished), a Sunday school, Church of England National School and school house.[7] Oddly, two Wesleyan Methodist chapels were built next to each other, because they sit either side of the Newstead/Annesley parish boundary on Tilford Road.

Housing & Amenities: The Twentieth Century

During the inter-war period Newstead was one of thirty five colliery villages developed by the Industrial Housing Association (IHA). This was an association of colliery company directors headed by Lord Aberconway and Arthur Markham, who had a vested interest in developments at Newstead: Aberconway and Markham's brother were company directors. By 1924 a total of 220 houses were built under the guidance of Sir John Tudor Walters as a company director of the IHA, who had set new national guidance with his report for central government.[8] As such this estate was built on a spacious geometric plan radiating from a new central axis and entrance along

References

4. H. Hay & D. Fordham, *New Coalfields, New Housing* (Fedj-el-Adoum, 2017), p.102.

5. 1881–1911 Census Records & 1939 Register, see: findmypast.co.uk

6. Bult 1875, see: *The Church History Project: A Guide to the Churches of Southwell and Nottingham Diocese* (2013), p.193.

7. Nottingham Insight Mapping, O/S Maps 1875–85, 1887–1899, 1912–1919 and 1937–40.

8. Sir John Tudor Walters, *Report of the Committee Appointed to Consider Questions of Building Construction in Connection with the Provision of Dwellings for the Working Classes* (1918).

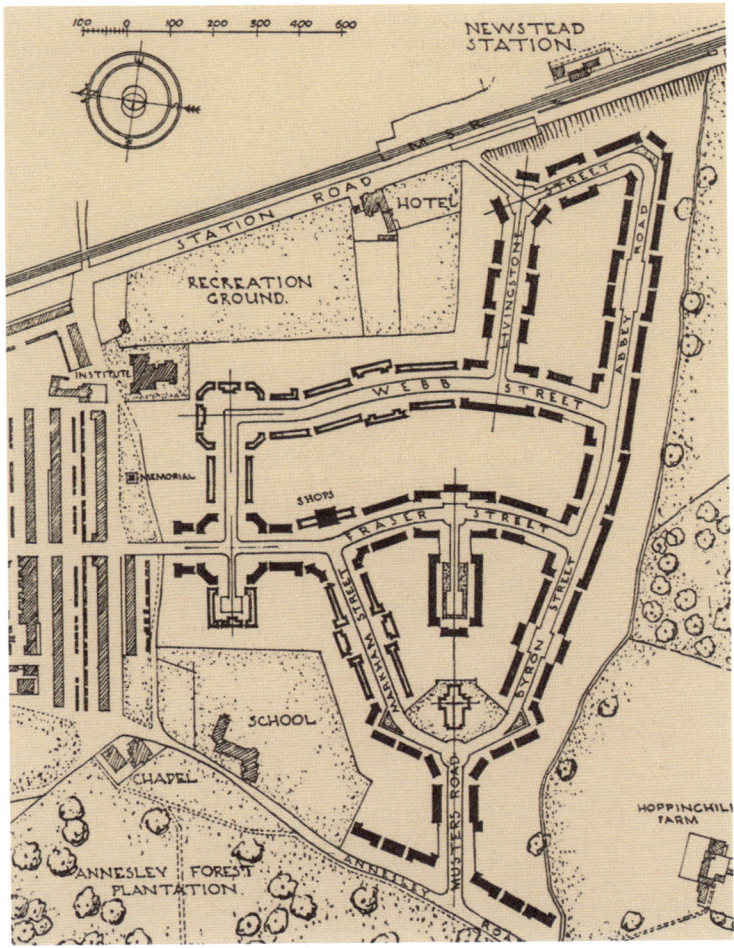

↑ Plans for a new model village at Newstead, circa early 1920s by the Industrial Housing Association. Notice how the new spacious geometric plan on the right contrasts with the old grid of narrow terraces on the left.
--
From J. T. Walters, *The Building of Twelve Thousand Houses* (Ernest Benn, 1927). Courtesy University of Nottingham Manuscripts and Special Collections, Oversize Em. G15 WAL

References

9. J. Tudor Walters, *The Building of Twelve Thousand Houses* (London, 1927).

10. Grade II listed, See: https://historicengland.org.uk/listing/the-list/list-entry/145511

11. *Tender*, Sheffield Daily Telegraph 11 July 1925, p.1. See: The British Newspaper Archive, online.

12. *The Church History Project: A Guide to the Churches of Southwell and Nottingham Diocese* (2013), p.193.

13. See website: www.nonstandardhouse.com/cornish-unit-type-1-precast-reinforced-concrete-house/

* **lancet**
a tall narrow window or aperture with a pointed arch at the top

Musters Road. The contrast in plan with the old Victorian terraces was deliberate. The new estate was greener and broader, with a diversity of house types to break monotony and create variation. Miners' houses were built with a bathroom which in most cases was positioned on the ground floor to limit the spread of coal dust.[9]

After the First World War a granite wheel-head cross was erected on Tilford Road in memorial to local service personnel.[10] The miners' institute was commissioned in 1925 by Newstead Miners' Welfare to accommodate a dance hall, stage, games room, lounge and bowling green. It was designed by architects Warner and Bocock of Sutton in Ashfield.[11] The building was modified in the 1970s and by 2000 a new conference centre was developed on the western side of the complex. This was to accompany Rural Community Action Notts (RCAN) which was launched to regenerate the Nottinghamshire coalfield but later abolished by the Cameron government.

At the central point of the new estate a new church was commissioned by the Church of England and erected by Hartley and Co in 1928. St Mary the Virgin was designed by the architect Cyril F. W. Hasledine in the Early English Gothic style with round-headed lancet* windows and large single span roof.[12]

The management structure of the colliery company was underpinned by the design of the new estate. The most spacious parlour type accommodation is located along Hucknall Road and was provided for the under managers and clerks. To the rear the housing was smaller, non-parlour but with a range of types, mostly three bed, semi-detached, and right angle plans for corner plots. As was common with IHA housing estates the perimeter walls were topped with round coping (said to keep maintenance costs down) and the entrance to the new estate was marked with pillars along Fraser Street. The road names reflected the history of the colliery ownership or the local landed elite; Markham, Abbey, Musters, Byron, Webb and Fraser. Livingstone may have been chosen in recollection of William Frederick Webb's meeting in Africa with the explorer David Livingstone.

Later Development

The estate was not completed according to its inter-war plan: 80 houses and a row of shops went unbuilt while Fraser Street never rejoined with Webb Street. Following nationalisation the gap sites on Markham Street were filled with housing built by the National Coal Board. They commissioned the popular Cornish Type houses which were manufactured with pre-cast concrete and designed by A. E. Beresford & R. Tonkin.[13] These buildings have since been rebuilt in brick but their distinctive mansard roofs remain. Following the closure of the colliery in 1987 and the subsequent demolition of its industrial plant, a red pit winding wheel was erected beside Station Avenue.

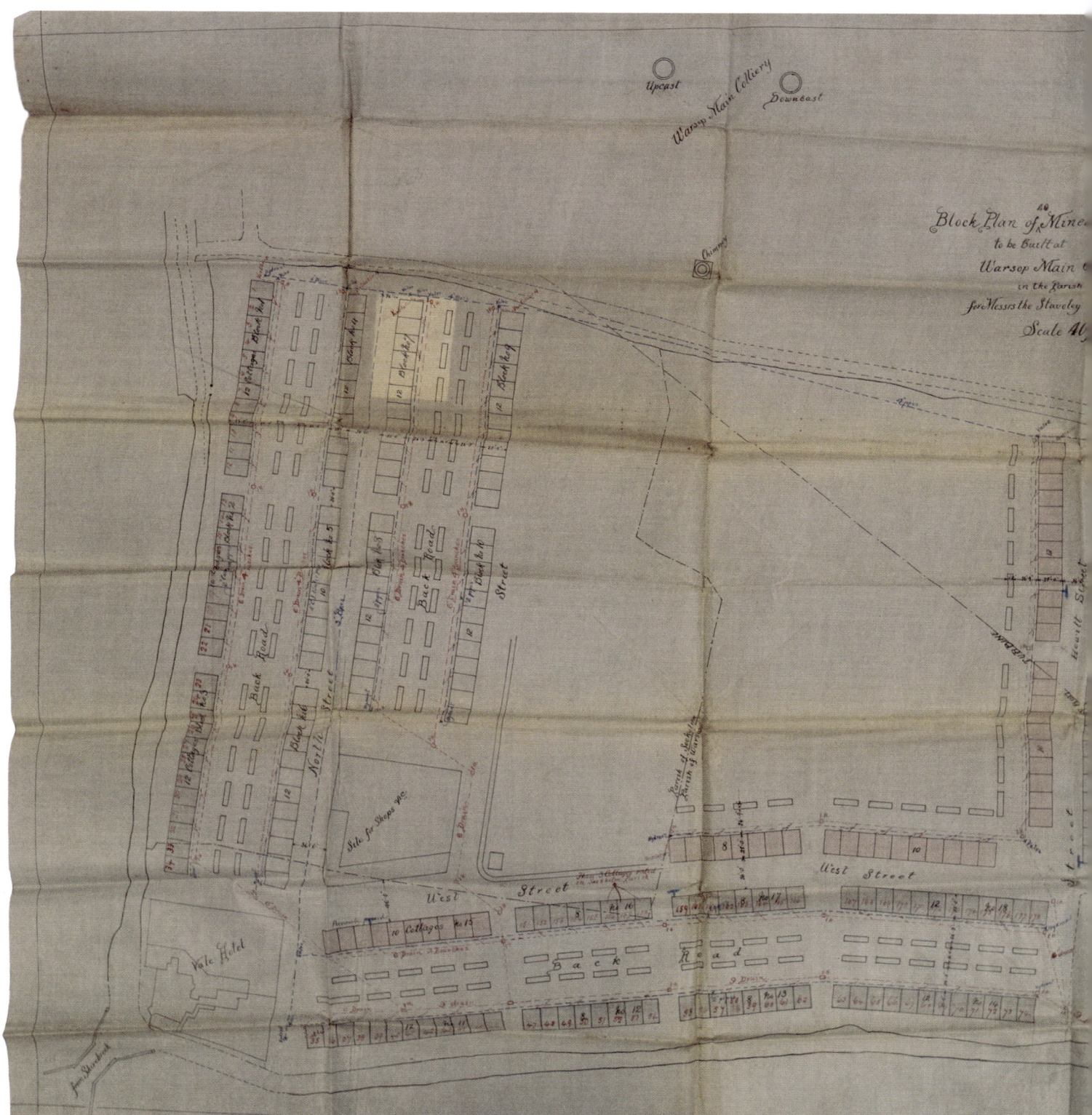

Warsop Main Colliery

Block Plan of Miners
to be Built at
Warsop Main
in the Parish
for Messrs the Staveley
Scale 40

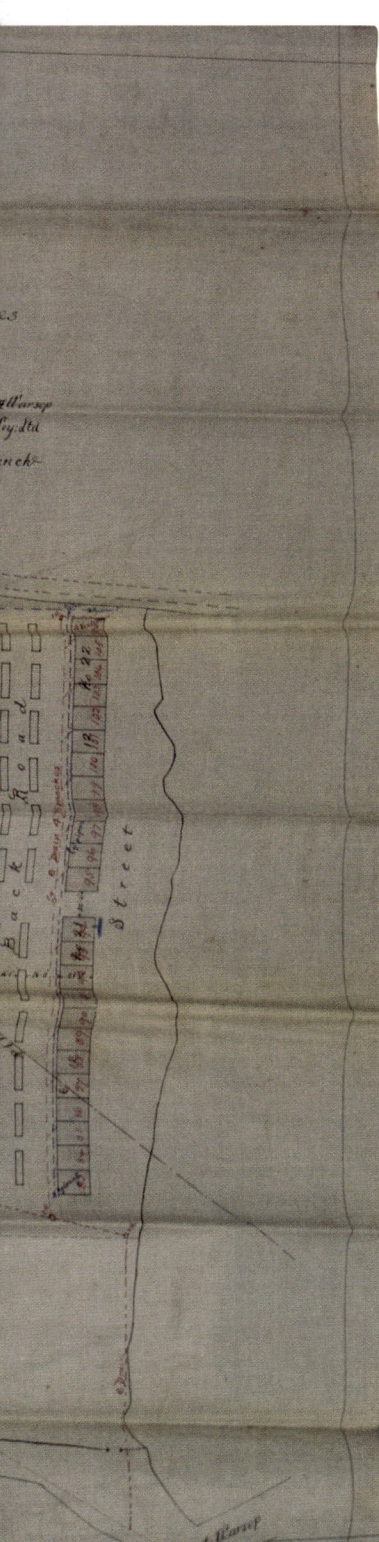

← Plan for a further 40 houses, Warsop Vale, for the Staveley Coal and Iron Company Ltd, 1907. Plan also shows houses already built, the privies between terraces, a site for shops and the Vale Hotel.

--

Courtesy Inspire Nottinghamshire Archives DC/WA/5/1/B127

References

1. Durham Mining Museum Website, www.dmm.org.uk

2. Nottinghamshire Archives, *Warsop Vale: Miners' cottages*, DC/WA/5/1/1/A30; Nottinghamshire Archives, *Warsop Vale: 40 houses*, DC/WA/5/1/1/B127.

3. Nottinghamshire Archives, *Warsop Vale: 40 houses*, DC/WA/5/1/1/B127. Also: www.warsopvale.org/history.htm

3. RENEWED PROSPERITY
Warsop & Mansfield: 1890–1919
Warsop Vale, Welbeck, Rufford

WARSOP VALE
Chris Matthews

Company & Village

Following on from their late nineteenth century success in establishing a series of large collieries in Yorkshire and Derbyshire, the Staveley Coal and Iron Company turned their attention towards the Mansfield district of Nottinghamshire. Developments such as Warsop Vale marked a period of renewed enterprise for the coal industry, following a temporary fall in demand in the mid 1870s. Here, land was leased from the Fitzherbert family of Nettleworth Hall and sinking commenced for Warsop Main Colliery in 1896. By 1923 it was by far and away Staveley's largest colliery, employing over 2,500 people and highly productive.[1] Along with Bolsover, Butterley and Stanton, the Staveley Coal and Iron Co had become one of the biggest companies operating in the East Midlands. Though it is possible that some of the buildings at Warsop were designed by Raymond Unwin (who from 1887–1896 was working as engineer for the Staveley Company), this has not been verified via archival plans. Unwin would later become a nationally influential figure in housing design, popularising the ideals of the garden city, particularly through his work at Letchwoth.[2]

Housing & Amenities

By 1914 the company had provided 220 terraced houses at Warsop Vale and like Newstead Colliery before it, they were generally characterised by blocks of terraces arranged along linear routes at right angles from Carter Lane. The houses had privies built as separate structures in the yards to the rear. They were built by Moore's from North Derbyshire at a cost of £40 per house. Each house consisted of two rooms downstairs (with a large pantry) and three bedrooms upstairs. By 1907 over 200 houses had been built and a further 40 were planned along Hewett Street and West Street.[3] A cricket ground was established at the centre of the village, which gives some indication that there was an attempt to create a model village square like Bolsover or Creswell. Two streets either side of the Malcolm Sargison Resource Centre (formally the Warsop Vale Co-operative) were never fully developed, while most of the original

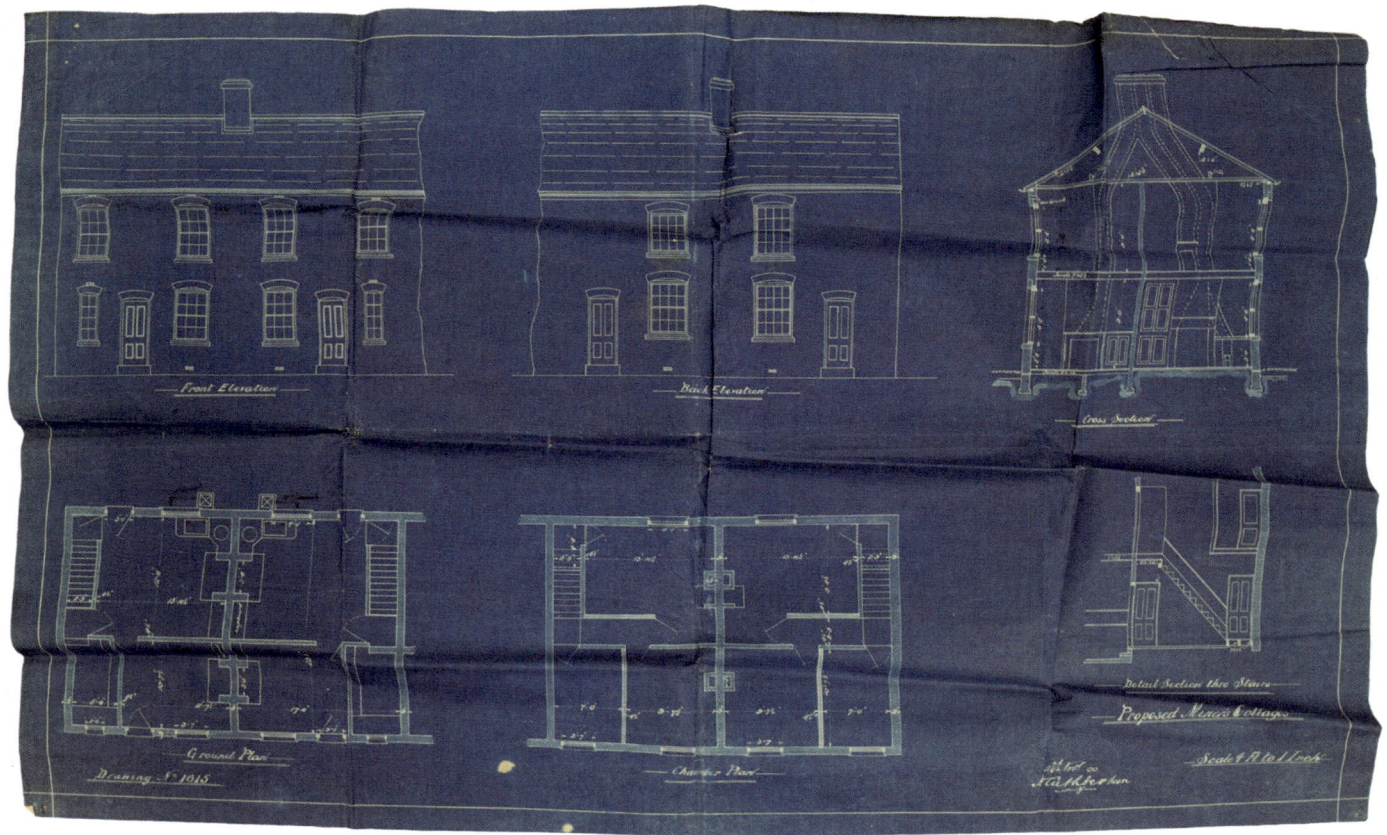

Hewett Street has since been demolished. Nevertheless, this was an established community with a variety of amenities. Some of these were built by the colliery company, such as a cricket pavilion, allotments, parsonage, school and co-op. Others were provided by separate organisations but with support from the colliery company such as the Primitive Methodist Chapel and Mission Church. The art nouveau Vale Hotel was planned in 1903 by the Staveley & District Public Houses Trust Ltd and featured a clubroom, 5 bedrooms, parlour, refreshment room, smoke room, kitchen and stable yard.[4]

Again like Newstead by the 1920s the Staveley Company was soliciting the services of the Industrial Housing Association (IHA), to build a large and very different estate to its Victorian predecessor. Unlike Newstead however its scale and location from the colliery were far more significant. One of the directors of the IHA was Arthur Markham, who had an interest in developments at Warsop via his Chairmanship of the Staveley Coal and Iron Co. By 1927 the development of a new estate with 477 houses was underway.[5] This was positioned a mile away from the original colliery village towards

↑ Plan for miners' cottages, Warsop Vale, 1900. These drawings show typical designs for two up two down terraced houses of this period.
--
Courtesy © Inspire Nottinghamshire Archives DC/WA/5/1/A30

References

4. The following have since been demolished: Primitive Methodist chapel, mission church, school and cricket pavilion. For the Vale Hotel see: Nottinghamshire Archives, *Warsop Vale: New hotel*, DC/WA/5/1/1/B72.

5. Nottinghamshire Archives, *Warsop: Layout of Warsop housing*, DC/WA/5/1/1/B414.

References

6. H. Hay & D. Fordham, *New Coalfields, New Housing* (Fedj-el-Adoum, 2017), p.124.

7. J. Tudor Walters, *The Building of Twelve Thousand Houses* (London, 1927).

8. 1881–1911 Census Records & 1939 Register. See: findmypast.co.uk

9. Nottinghamshire Archives, *Wood Lane, Warsop: Institute*, DC/WA/5/1/B446.

10. Nottingham Journal, *Institute for Worksop*, 03 January 1933.

11. D. Waddington, (Policy Press, 2003), p.51.

12. Meden Valley Making Places (MVMP), Market Warsop, Nottinghamshire, see: www.oneeastmidlands.org.uk/sites/default/files/library/medenvalley.pdf

↓ Proposed designs for Laurel Street at Warsop Vale by the Industrial Housing Association, c.1927.

--

From J. T. Walters, *The Building of Twelve Thousand Houses* (Ernest Benn, 1927). Courtesy University of Nottingham Manuscripts and Special Collections, Oversize Em. G15 WAL

Church Warsop and planned on a loose grid roughly following the contours of the slope. Roads took their names from trees and shrubs and houses were positioned to take advantage of the south facing sunlight. This was particularity the case with Poplar Grove, while others such as Laurel Avenue were originally arranged around a communal garden square with a central sundial.[6] The ethos of the IHA housing schemes can be seen throughout: broken frontage lines, preserving natural features and a variety of elevations and house types, including cottage shops and corner houses.[7]

The colliery management were accommodated in houses built prior to 1914. These houses were positioned at a distance from the miners' houses but in sight of the colliery. Herbert Grant, the Colliery Manager, was residing in a large detached house called Rock House off Carter Lane.[8] Nearby, the under managers and senior engineers were living at Rock Cottages, a row of 6 houses also known as 'Rhein o' Thorns' and built in local Magnesium Limestone. The company had also built a parsonage on Carter Lane south of the railway line. The colliery deputies generally neighboured the miners in the terraces of North Lane and Carter Lane.

With management already provided for, the IHA development was subsequently less hierarchical than some of its contemporaries but there were still some important differences in scale and house type. The only detached house on the new estate was intended as a surgery and positioned on the corner of Birch Lane and Wood Lane. It was given special treatment via large bay windows on both floors and entablature* above the ground floor entrance. The semi-detached houses immediately north-west of the surgery appear to have been the most desirable location for the deputies and engineers. The rest of the housing was generally smaller but with a variety of types; semi-detached, right angle plans for corner plots, cottage shops (on the corner of Sycamore Street and Laurel Avenue) and a nurse's bungalow (at the end of Birch St). As was common with IHA housing estates, brick walls form the garden perimeter, while an allotment or playground was earmarked at the rear of houses along Laurel Avenue and Sycamore Street. Facing the estate on Wood Lane is a bowling green, football field and institute, which was provided by the Warsop Main Miners' Welfare Committee. Plans were submitted in 1929 and the building was complete by 1933.[9] The neo-Tudor design was in accordance with the neighbouring housing but conducted by the architects Warner and Dean of Sutton in Ashfield.[10]

Following the closure of the colliery in 1989, The Malcolm Sargison Resource Centre formed the centre of the regeneration programme where the non-profit company Meden Vale Making Places Ltd, was set up to tackle run down and empty properties.[11] It has since purchased 800 properties in north Nottinghamshire and north-east Derbyshire.[12]

* entablature
horizontal moldings located above the columns of a classical structure

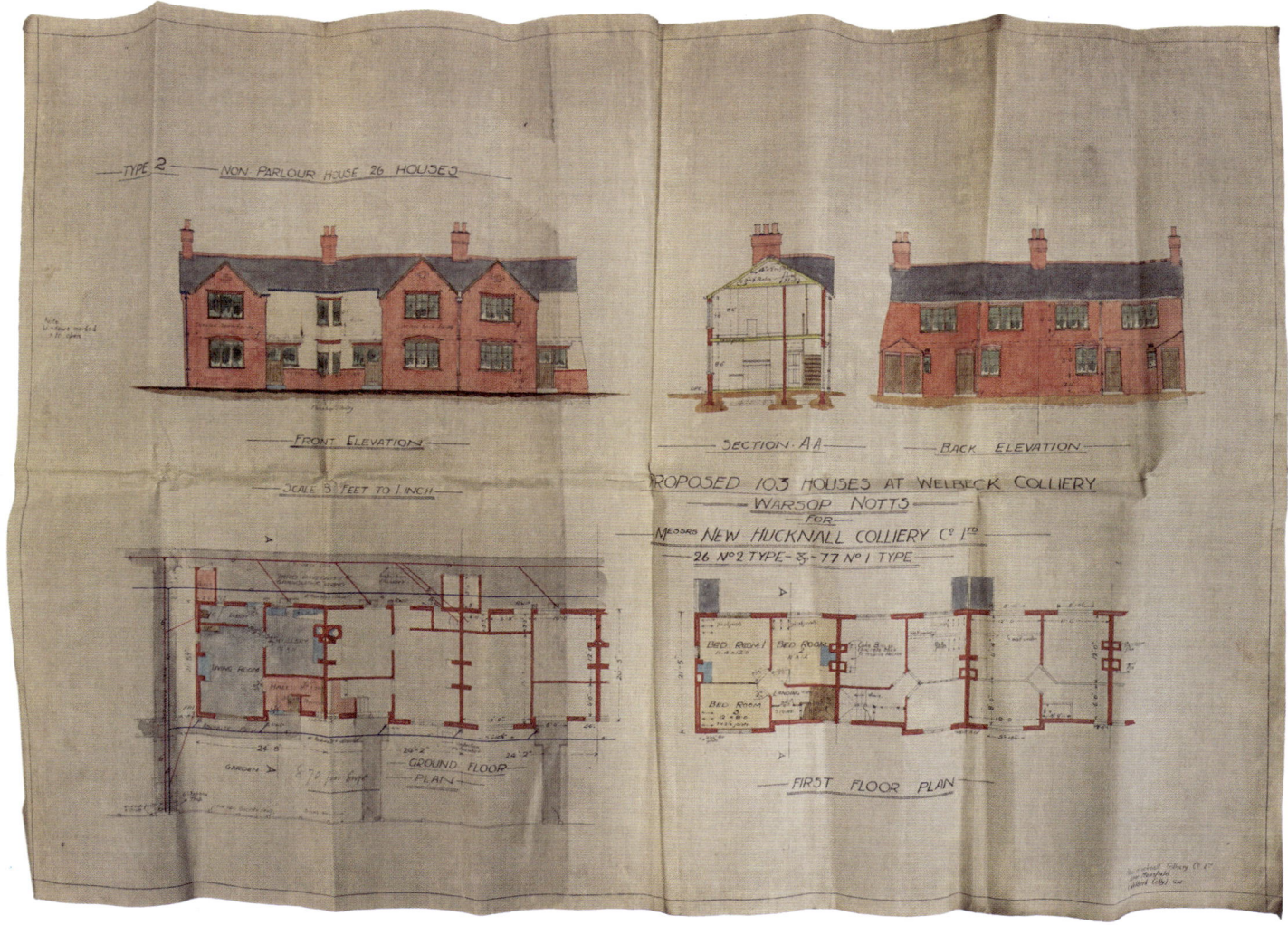

WELBECK COLLIERY VILLAGE (MEDEN VALE)
Chris Matthews

Company & Village

Welbeck Colliery Village was initiated by a company of mining entrepreneurs from the North East keen to take advantage of the concealed Nottinghamshire coalfield. Emerson Muschamp Bainbridge was one of the founding directors and also established the Bolsover Colliery Company. His earlier company, however, was named after New Hucknall in Nottinghamshire, where the firm established their first colliery 1874–1876.[1] Welbeck was to be their third and was named after the Welbeck estate belonging to the Duke of Portland who leased the required land to the New Hucknall Colliery Company. Both parties had already established a successful working relationship in the Mansfield district of Nottinghamshire,

↑ Plan for 113 houses at Welbeck Colliery by the architect George Warner for the New Hucknall Colliery Company, 1926.
--
Courtesy Inspire Nottinghamshire Archives DC/WA/5/1/C34

References

1. Durham Mining Museum Website, www.dmm.org.uk

↓ Proposed layout for a mining village at Welbeck Colliery, Warsop, Nottinghamshire, by George Warner for the New Hucknall Colliery Company, 1920. George Warner was also responsible for designing a number of Miners' Welfares in the Nottinghamshire coalfield.

--

Courtesy Inspire Nottinghamshire Archives DC/WA/5/1/B270

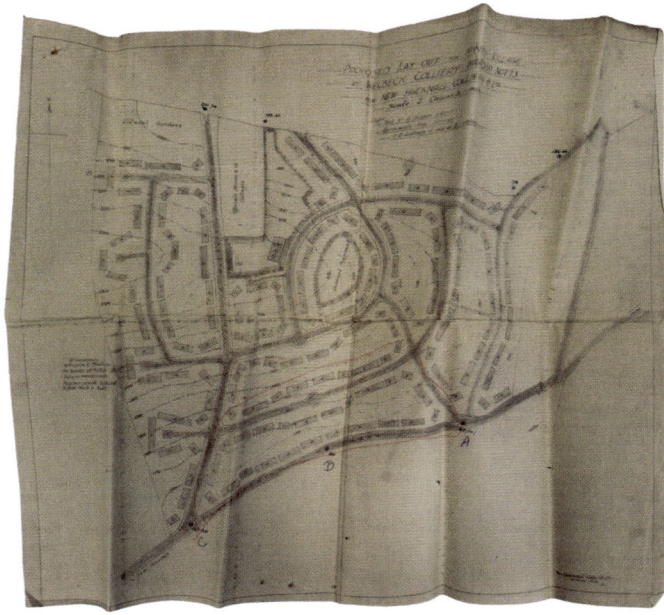

* facing gables
triangular portion of a wall between roof pitch, which faces the street or entrance

References

2. A. R. Griffin, *Mining in the East Midlands, 1550–1947* (Frank Cass, 1971), p.168; Nottinghamshire Archives, *Welbeck Colliery: Layout for New Mining Village*, DC/WA/5/1/B270.

3. *The Church History Project: A Guide to the Churches of Southwell and Nottingham Diocese* (online), see: https://southwellchurches.nottingham. ac.uk/meden-vale/

4. In 1939 the colliery manager's gardener was Robert W Askey who lived at 17 Budby Crescent, see 1939 Register, findmypast.co.uk

profiting from increased demand at the turn of the century. Sinking commenced at Welbeck in 1912 and by 1933 it was home to a large colliery employing more than 1,500 people. The village itself was small when compared to its contemporaries though 60% of its housing stock was built in the neighbouring town of Market Warsop. In the 1960s it was renamed Meden Vale, after the River Meden that runs south of Netherfield Lane

Housing

The ambition of the New Hucknall Colliery Company was emphasised by their commitment to building housing for their employees. Between 1912 and 1928 the company built a grand total of 877 houses, most of which were designed by George Warner of Sutton in Ashfield.[2] Of these around half were constructed in the neighboring town of Market Warsop. Here, development began on Clumber Street and eventually stretched half a mile south to the company cricket ground on Oakfield Lane. Many of these houses were complete by 1922 and predate Welbeck Colliery Village. The streets were planned along linear routes and right angles, while roads were named after company directors (Fenwick, Muschamp and Bainbridge) and their successful enterprises (Welbeck, Bentinck). Houses were a mixture of basic terraces and those with more decorative features. The roads between Muschamp Terrace and Newcastle Street were more desirable; with slightly larger houses, facing gables* and hallways, some of which faced a bowling green. Later developments towards Morven Terrace were more spaciously planned with both front and back gardens and a mixture of types.

The first houses of Welbeck Colliery Village were built for management and constructed 1912–22. They were located adjacent to the entrance to the colliery along Elkesley Road. The rest of the estate was intended for the miners and consisted of around 300 houses, built 1924–26. It was planned along radial routes and positioned at a fair distance from management. Close to the central axis of the plan a mission church was erected in 1929–30 with financial support from the New Hucknall Colliery Co. It was dedicated to St Hilda and described at the time as 'a simple brick building [with] a bright and pleasing interior' and designed by George Warner.[3] Attendance declined in the post-war period, and the church was closed by the mid-1970s and later demolished.

As was typical with colliery villages in the concealed coalfield the individual size of each house was characterised by the chain of command at the colliery. The manager resided at Elkesley House, a large detached building with a generous garden and full height perimeter brick wall. Upkeep necessitated the employment of a colliery manager's gardener.[4] The under managers resided next door at a pair of large semi-detached houses called Beechwood Villas, equipped with shaped entablature above the entrance and generous gardens to the rear. Colliery deputies, skilled miners and senior engineers lived in two rows of six terraces to the north of

Beechwood Villas, planned along a right angle between Elkesley Road and Elkesley Place. These were designed with hallways, ground floor bay windows and shaped entablature surrounding the entrances. The miners' houses between Budby Crescent and Netherfield Lane were generally less decorated, but still built to a good standard. Here, there were two types of interlocking houses; parlour and non-parlour with facing gables.[5] These were generally planned in groups of four or six along straight routes but also two on corner plots to create variation. All had three bedrooms, water closets, bath in scullery and rear coal shed.

Amenities

By the late 1920s a variety of amenities had been provided and were positioned in a relatively unplanned fashion, away from the estate to the east of Elkesley Road. In 1924 the County Council took the decision to build Netherfield Lane School (now Eastlands).[6] This was built in a brick classical style with occasional render and clay roof tiles. The Institute was commissioned by Welbeck Colliery Miners' Welfare in 1939 to replace an earlier temporary structure. This new building was designed by the architects Warner and Dean of Sutton in Ashfield, to house a main hall with stage, dressing room and dance hall.[7] The school, Methodist chapel, surgery and police house were built by associated organisations separate from the colliery company. To the west along Prest Avenue, is a large former retail building, which was occupied by the Mansfield & Sutton Co-operative Society. It was later converted to a house, but retains some of the original features such as the first floor loading bay.[8] The Welbeck Colliery Sports and Recreation Club also commissioned a sports pavilion along Sherwood Street in neighbouring Warsop and plans were submitted in 1928. This was a single story arts and crafts building with a dormer window in the attic.[9] The site has recently been demolished and cleared for housing.

Later Developments

After the Second World War the village was extended to the west with a mixture of housing built by the local authority and private developers. Nottinghamshire County Council subsequently built Netherfield Infant School using their prefabricated modernist CLASP system, finished with hung tiles. Opposite the school on Netherfield Lane is the Three Lions pub. This was built around the 1960s by Mansfield Brewery in the Scandinavian modernist style. In June 2021 it was under threat of demolition.[10]

↑ Welbeck Colliery headstocks and village, 1975.
--
Courtesy © Chad newspaper, photography by Roger Grayson

References

5. Nottinghamshire Archives, *Welbeck Colliery: 100 houses*, DC/WA/5/1/1/B292; Nottinghamshire Archives, *Welbeck Colliery, Warsop: Plan 2 for 113 houses*, DC/WA/5/1/1/C34.

6. Nottingham Journal, *Welbeck's New Pithead Baths*, 17 June 1939.

7. Nottinghamshire Archives, *Warsop: Eastlands School, 1924–1954*, SCH/179/7.

8. See: www.signsofthepast.org.uk

9. Nottinghamshire Archives, *Sherwood Street, Warsop: Sports pavilion*, DC/WA/5/1/B444.

10. Mansfield Chad, *Plans to demolish struggling pub near Mansfield and build almost 50 affordable homes*, 22/06/21.

John Plowright Houfton was General Manager of the company from 1911 until his death in 1929. He oversaw the development of model villages at Forest Town, Rainworth, Clipstone and Edwinstowe. His cousin Percy Bond Houfton worked as an architect for the company.

--

From: *Bolsover Jubilee Souvenir, 1889–1939*, (Bolsover Colliery Company, 1939). Courtesy University of Nottingham Manuscripts and Special Collections, Oversize Em. O46 BOL

Rainworth Colliery, c.1939.

--

From: *Bolsover Jubilee Souvenir, 1889–1939*, (Bolsover Colliery Company, 1939). Courtesy University of Nottingham Manuscripts and Special Collections, Oversize Em. O46 BOL

RUFFORD (RAINWORTH)
Chris Matthews

Company & Village

On the eve of nationalisation the Bolsover Colliery Company was the third most successful colliery company in the country.[1] Key to that success was the string of collieries the company established in the East Midlands; Bolsover (1889), Creswell (1894–1896), Forest Town (aka Crown Farm, 1904 -1905), Rufford (1911–1913), Clipstone (1919), and Thoresby (1925).[2] Each of which was equipped with model villages, and Creswell is arguably the most laudable. Rufford colliery was the Bolsover company's second mine to be established within the Mansfield district. Perhaps more than any other company Bolsover absorbed the aesthetics of the arts & crafts, but with equal vigour stamped out the political ethos associated with that movement. A pit wheel memorial to the colliery now stands beside the former entrance on Kirklington Road.

References

1. Phillip Riden, *The Bolsover Colliery Company*, VCH, see: https://www.victoriacountyhistory.ac.uk/explore/items/bolsover-colliery-company

2. Durham Mining Museum Website, www.dmm.org.uk

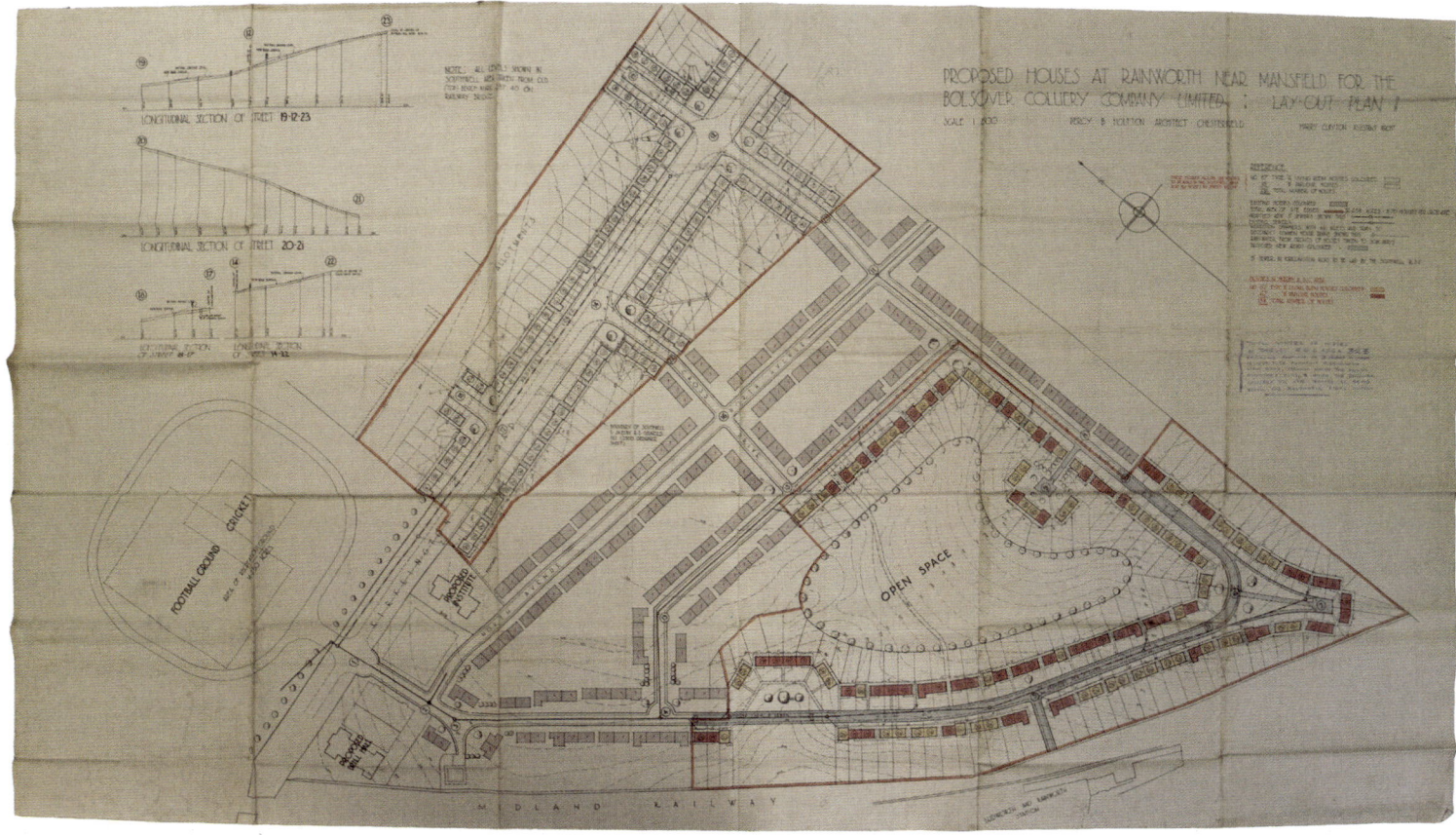

Housing

Prior to Rufford Colliery, Bolsover's success had been based on securing leases from the Duke of Portland. At Rainworth however Bolsover worked with a new client, Lord Savile, and so the colliery was named after Savile's Rufford estate. Although the colliery was partly located in the Mansfield Town District, most of the housing and colliery was positioned just over the border and came under the authority of Skegby Rural District Council. The first houses were located on the Mansfield side on Southwell Road East and built 1912–19.[3] The planning and architectural details were similar to the Bolsover company's previous undertaking in Mansfield at Forest Town; a grid of approximately 128 cottage style houses between First and Fourth Avenue, with front and back gardens and occasional variation marked with facing gables, pantiles and dog toothed lintels* supporting the chimney stacks at end terraces. It is likely therefore that like Forest Town, these houses were designed by Percy Bond Houfton with a rear pan closet toilet and no bathroom.[4]

↑ Plan showing proposed housing scheme at Rainworth near Mansfield for The Bolsover Colliery Co Ltd, 1920. Notice how the entrance to the sports field forms a neat axis with the entrance to the estate between the Drill Hall and Institute. Sport and organised social activities had an important role to play in creating company loyalty. Also: the red blocks denote relatively spacious houses with a parlour, while yellow locates the smaller and more affordable non-parlour houses. This document shows how the Bolsover Colliery Company liked to create mixed housing estates.
--
Courtesy Nottinghamshire Archives, DC/SW/4/8/23/1

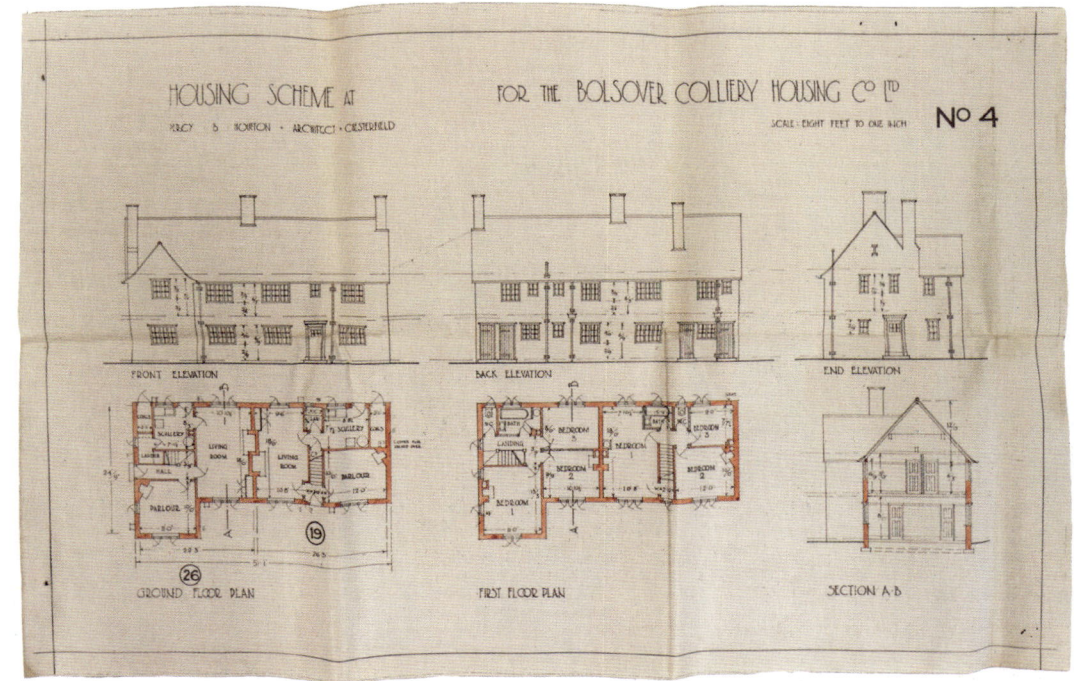

→ House Type 4 by the Bolsover Colliery Company for Rainworth model village, 1923. This design shows a spacious parlour house with three bedrooma and an upstairs bathroom.
--
Courtesy Nottinghamshire Archives, DC/SW/4/8/23/4

References

3. Nottingham Insight Mapping, O/S Maps, 1912–1919.

4. P. Marples, *Forest Town: The village that grew out of coal* (Forest Town Heritage Group, 2005); pp.27–32.

5. R. J. Waller, *The Dukeries Transformed: The Social and Political Development of a Twentieth Century Coalfield* (Clarendon Press, 1983), p.27.

6. VCH Explore, *The Houftons*, see: www.victoriacountyhistory.ac.uk/explore/items/houftons

7. A. R. Griffin, Mining in the East Midlands, 1550–1947 (Frank Cass, 1971), p.12.

8. A. R. Griffin, *Mining in the East Midlands, 1550–1947* (Frank Cass, 1971), p.266

* pantile
a type of fired roof tile, normally made from clay and S-shaped in profile

By 1931 the population of Rainworth had more than doubled in the space of 10 years to 894 people.[5] This was a consequence of further house building activities by the Bolsover Colliery Company, who built approximately 400 houses to the east of the Mansfield Urban District border, in a triangle plot between Kirklington Road, Python Hill Road and South Avenue. Given the scale of the development Rainworth was nicknamed 'White City' after the famous international exhibition site in North London. Following new national housing guidelines set out in the Tudor Walters Report, these were more spaciously planned with larger gardens, wider roads and more green space. The architectural details were similar to those on Southwell Road East, such as the steep pitch of the roof designed for supporting pantiles*. However, the overall effect of this estate was more varied with two types of roof tile, brick air vents and entrance entablatures. The geometric plan and housing design was designed by the architect, Percy Bond Houfton with Harry Clayton working as his assistant. Houfton's cousin John Plowright Houfton was General Manager of the company from 1911 until his death in 1929.[6]

In 1913 during sinking operations 14 lives were lost when a heavy water barrel accidently fell down the shaft, killing the sinkers.[7] The disaster at Rufford highlighted the risks associated with mining and the necessity for diligent conduct. Despite this setback Rufford Colliery was a highly successful enterprise and often at the forefront in mining techniques, such as breaking record outputs in 1933 with a double unit conveyor system.[8]

References

9. 1939 Register. See: findmypast.co.uk

10. Nottinghamshire Archives, *Plan showing proposed housing scheme at Rainworth*, DC/SW/4/8/23/1.

11. Mansfield Reporter, *Cornish Miners' Concert Party at Primitive Methodist School Hall*, 08 June 1923, p.8; Mansfield Reporter, *Drill Hall, Rainworth*, 04 November 1927, p.5.

12. Nottinghamshire Archives, *Plans of The Picture House*, CC/CL/2/5/2/40.

← Garden city style housing by the Bolsover Colliery Company, Kirklington Road.
--
Courtesy © Chris Matthews

Success generated secure employment, high wages and company loyalty; in 1936 Rufford had the highest membership of the breakaway Nottingham Miners' Industrial Union (aka 'Spencer Union'). This was a non-political union that had broken away from the Miners' Federation of Great Britain in the autumn of 1926 during the latter stages of the 1926 Miners' Lockout.

That loyalty was underpinned by the company's shrewd management of its tied housing; if tenants' upkeep was negligent they stood to lose their house and job. Evictions were conducted swiftly. This top down approach was reinforced in the layout of the housing estate, with managers residing close to the colliery 1½ miles to the north of the village at Elmsley Villas.[9] These houses have since been demolished but it appears they were older tenant farm houses belonging to Lord Savile. Census records suggest that colliery deputies mixed with hewers on each street. Parlour and non-parlour houses were also mixed throughout the estate and were mostly 3 bed with an upstairs bathroom.[10]

Amenities

During the 1920s Rainworth experienced a significant improvement in the standard of amenities conducive to village life with a new school (Python Hill), drill hall, Methodist chapel and recreation ground in place by the late 1920s.[11] Rainworth Picture House could seat 400 people and was designed in 1920 by W. W. Wheatley.[12]

↑ Original 1920s features still intact on Python Hill Road, Rainworth.
--
Courtesy © Chris Matthews

Sports and social activities appear to have been planned at an axis to the entrance of the estate on South Avenue. This is a neat example of how sports were an essential part of the Bolsover colliery company ethos. Building dates are difficult to ascertain but certainly by the late 1930s the village had acquired a new Miners' Welfare on North Avenue (later extended in the post-war period) and the Robin Hood Inn had been upgraded to accommodate more customers.[13] The Church of St Simon & St Jude on Southwell Road East was complete in 1939 to the designs of Claude Howitt of Nottingham.[14] The overall effect is an attractive mix of Romanesque and Art Deco motifs, soldier courses, Flemish bond brickwork, orange tiles and bell turret.[15] Python Hill School was built in 1925 by Nottinghamshire County Council.[16] This building is designed in a brick classical style on a quadrangle plan with pitched roofs and slate tiles.

Later Developments

After the Second World War the village was extended to the south, east and west with a mixture of private and local authority housing. The County Council provided a large school complex on Warsop Lane using their prefabricated modernist CLASP system. It has since been reclad. On the perimeter of the village there are two twentieth century pubs of note, The Archer on Warsop Lane and The Sherwood Inn on Kirklington Road, both of which combine modernist and traditional styles, with pitched roofs and generous ground floor windows.

↓ The Robin Hood Inn, Rainworth. There was an older pub on this site of the same name before it was rebuilt during the inter-war period. The design and scale of the building is similar to the Plough Inn at Ollerton and is likely to have been designed by the same architect, Aubrey Lane.
--
Courtesy Inspire Picture Archive & Reg Baker

→ The church of Rainworth St Jude and St Simon, built in 1929 and designed by Claude Howitt. The building features some excellent brickwork and a pleasing repetition of semi-octagonal arches.
--
Courtesy © Chris Matthews

References

13. Nottingham Insight Mapping, *O/S Maps, 1912–1919 and 1937–40*; Nottingham Evening Post, *Rainworth Working Men's Club*, 31.1.39, p.2.

14. *The Church History Project: A Guide to the Churches of Southwell and Nottingham Diocese* (2013), p.233.

15. C. Hartwell, N. Pevsner, E, Williamson *The Buildings of England: Nottinghamshire* (Yale, 2020), p.551.

16. *Nottinghamshire Archives, Rainworth; Python Hill School, 1925 – 1970,* SCH/199/1.

→ Clipstone Colliery from Vicar Water
  pond, 1968. In the 1870s this tributary
  of the River Maun was developed
  as a lake by the Duke of Portland. It
  was used as a trout fishery for the
  Duke's estate at Welbeck. After the
  development of Clipstone Colliery
  in 1922 fishing became popular
  with miners and the Duke awarded
  fishing rights to the Clipstone Colliery
  Angling Club.
  --
  Courtesy © Chad newspaper,
  photography by Roger Grayson

4. A SPECTACULAR MOMENT
The Dukeries & Sherwood Forest: 1920–1939, Clipstone, Thoresby, Bilsthorpe, Blidworth, Ollerton, Calverton

↑ Clipstone Colliery headstocks, the most impressive site in the Nottinghamshire coalfield and Grade II listed in 2000.

--

Courtesy © Chris Matthews

References

1. Sir Neil Cossons, 'Crazy for Clipstone' in *The National Association of Mining History Organisations, No. 70*, 2014.

2. R. J. Waller, *The Dukeries Transformed: The Social and Political Development of a Twentieth Century Coalfield* (Clarendon Press, 1983), p.4.

3. Sir Neil Cossons, 'Crazy for Clipstone' in *The National Association of Mining History Organisations, No. 70*, 2014.

4. Sir Neil Cossons, 'Crazy for Clipstone' in *The National Association of Mining History Organisations, No. 70*, 2014.

5. C. Hartwell, N. Pevsner, E, Williamson *The Buildings of England: Nottinghamshire* (Yale, 2020), p.179.

6. Nottingham Journal, *New Notts Colliery*, 14.8.15, p.3.

7. R. J. Waller, *The Dukeries Transformed: The Social and Political Development of a Twentieth Century Coalfield* (Clarendon Press, 1983), pp.27 & 79.

NEW CLIPSTONE
Chris Matthews

Company & Village

While Rufford was being sunk, the Bolsover Colliery Company was busy securing a new lease at Clipstone from the Duke of Portland.[1] This was the first of three collieries along the Maun valley in Sherwood Forest and as such it is an archetypal Dukeries coalfield village. Sinking operations were interrupted by the First World War and coal was finally won in 1922.[2] Nevertheless Clipstone became one of the most productive mines in Britain and still presents the best surviving example of twentieth century coal mining technology.[3] It was also home to Bolsover's largest colliery village. The headstocks and powerhouse were listed at Grade II in 2000 in recognition of their historical and architectural significance.

The Headstocks

More than any other structure the headstocks at Clipstone express the sheer productivity of the Nottinghamshire coalfield. Following nationalisation the colliery was modernised by the National Coal Board, between 1950–53, in order to extract coal from much deeper levels. The new shafts at Clipstone were among the deepest in the country; extending 1006 yards into the earth.[4] When built the headstocks were the tallest and most advanced in Europe. They were designed by the architects Young and Purves and built by Head Wrightson Colliery Engineering.[5] Between the latticework steel towers is the central modernist brick powerhouse which contains two Koepe winding engines. The 'Koepe' system was originally a late nineteenth century German invention rarely adopted in Britain but finally perfected at Clipstone.

Housing

In 1914 the plan for Clipstone was simply to extend Bolsover's older colliery village at Forest Town rather than build a new community.[6] However the realities of securing a regular supply of labour must have forced the company to reconsider their plans. During the 1920s the company erected 648 houses and by 1931 the population of the village had grown six fold in the space of ten years to 3443 people.[7]

← Church Road, Clipstone, c.1920s. Photograph taken by John Henry Spree, a Nottinghamshire photographer.
--
Courtesy Dave Fordham

↑ Mansfield Road, Clipstone, 1970. This photograph shows 'The Cottages' beneath the colliery headstocks. These houses were built for colliery company workers with managerial occupations.
--
Courtesy © Chad newspaper, photography by Roger Grayson

The original geometric plan and earliest housing was designed by the architects Houfton & Kington. The rectilinear plan form of the estate was broken by an oval circus at the centre and occasional crescents and cul-de-sacs setback from linear routes. Houfton had previously designed New Bolsover, Creswell and Rainworth, and his cousin was the general manager of the company until 1929. His garden city style housing was characterised by steep pitches for supporting pantiles, contrasting roof tiles, facing gables with air vents and entrance entablature.

Unlike Rainworth, the housing for colliery management has survived. These large semi-detached houses with spacious gardens were deliberately positioned on Mansfield Road either side of the colliery entrance. To the east are 'The Villas' in two pairs, numbered 1–7, and to the west 'The Cottages', in four pairs numbed 41–55. By 1939 these buildings housed a variety of managerial occupations including colliery manager, chief superintendent, overman, surveyor and chief electrician.[8] Like Rainworth it appears that colliery deputies generally mixed with hewers on each street, yet there was some preference for Forest Road and Mansfield Road.

Amenities

Some of the amenities necessary for community life were positioned towards the middle of a geometric plan. At the central entrance beside Fourth Avenue is the Miners' Institute, which was opened in 1933 and financed by the District Welfare Committee.[9] Built to accommodate 420 members the building was equipped with an impressive range of facilities including library, reading room, concert room, sun room, kitchen, bar, billiards room and bowling green. Adjacent to this is the Village Hall, which was commissioned by the Bolsover Colliery Company and built in 1935 to house a main hall, dance floor, balcony, gymnasium, stage, dressing rooms and kitchen.[10] Both these buildings exhibit motifs familiar with the arts and crafts movement and were designed by the architect G. Warner who had worked on similar schemes throughout the region.[11]

References

8. 1939 Register, see: findmypast.co.uk

9. Nottingham Journal, *New Miners' Institute: Fine Building at Clipstone*, 04 December 1933, p.7.

10. Nottingham Evening Post, *New Village Hall*, 14 June 1935, p.7, Nottingham Journal, *Clipstone Ceremony*, 15 June 1935, p.5.

11. Nottingham Journal, *New Village Hall*, 17 June 1935, p.5.

↓ Clipstone village hall interior.
--
From: *Bolsover Jubilee Souvenir, 1889–1939*, (Bolsover Colliery Company, 1939). Courtesy University of Nottingham Manuscripts and Special Collections, Oversize Em. O46 BOL

→ Clipstone village hall on the left. On the right is the Miners' Institute, c.1939. Both buildings were designed by the architect G. Warner who was a prolific architect for the colliery companies of the East Midlands.
--
From: *Bolsover Jubilee Souvenir, 1889–1939*, (Bolsover Colliery Company, 1939). Courtesy University of Nottingham Manuscripts and Special Collections, Oversize Em. O46 BOL

* cat slide roof
a section of a roof that is extended below the main height of the eaves

References

12. *The Church History Project: A Guide to the Churches of Southwell and Nottingham Diocese* (2013), p.81

13. Nottinghamshire Archives, *Clipstone Samuel Barlow School*, SCH/38/1.

14. R. J. Waller, T*he Dukeries Transformed: The Social and Political Development of a Twentieth Century* (Clarendon Press, 1983), p.90.

15. Nottinghamshire Archives, P*lans of Ritz Cinema, Mansfield Road, Clipstone*, CC/CL/2/5/2/91.

Beyond these buildings is a central playing field originally with a Methodist chapel to the west, which was built in 1927 and since demolished. To the east was the more impressive neo-Romanesque All Saints' Church, which was designed by Louis Ambler and built in 1928. This was financed chiefly by the Bolsover Colliery Company with significant contributions from the Duke of Portland, the Marquis of Titchfield and the Ecclesiastical Commissioners.[12] Ambler was working with familiar clients, having previously designed St Alban's at Forest Town and St Winifred's Church at Holbeck near Worksop. Inside the church is a large piece of coal and set of kneelers, both of which act as memorials to the colliery. The adjacent vicarage is the largest detached house on the estate, built with facing gables, rear garage and a cat slide roof* above the central entrance. Further east along Church Road the Samuel Barlow School was built in 1926 by Nottinghamshire County Council.[13] The building is in a brick classical style on a quadrangle plan with pitched roofs and clay tiles.

Like Ollerton and Blidworth the shopping district is the only irregular layout of the inter-war period. The colliery company leased plots of land for retail developments, which prospective traders built themselves.[14] In the case of Clipstone this was along Mansfield Road and here the most interesting structure was the Ritz Cinema (recently demolished), which was built in 1937 and designed in the Art Deco style by Mansfield architects Bocock and Kirk.[15]

Later Developments

After the Second World War the village was extended with a mixture of council and private housing to the east and west of the original housing. Nottinghamshire County Council provided a series of new schools, using the prefabricated modernist CLASP system. Garabaldi School is a large complex built using concrete panels, while Newlands Junior School and Sherwood East are both faced with hung tiles.

BILSTHORPE
Clare Hartwell & Chris Matthews

Company & Village

Before the arrival of the colliery Bilsthorpe was a small agricultural village with medieval origins.[1] In 1925 the Stanton Ironworks Company began sinking a pit to the north of the old village on land leased from Lord Savile of Rufford. A brickyard was started on the site providing material for the works and housing. Part of the Old Rectory opposite the church was taken over as offices by the company. Stanton was a highly regarded industrial concern from near Ilkeston (Derbyshire), which was established in 1855 and had one of the largest pipe foundries in the country. The company sunk its first collieries at Teversal (1868) and Silverhill (1875), which necessitated a new mining village called Stanton Hill. A little later they were pioneering the exploitation of the concealed coalfield to the north of Mansfield at Pleasley.[2] Stanton Hill and Pleasley bare similar architectural characteristics to the inter-war buildings at Bilsthorpe, though these places were considerably less isolated. More building took place at Bilsthorpe after the Second World War, and the colliery eventually closed in 1997. The colliery buildings were demolished and a business park has been developed on part of the site. Oddly, the pumphouse survived. This was formally used to transfer colliery water to the lagoons.

↓ Savile Road, Bilsthorpe. This was considered to be one of the more desirable roads to live on for miners who wanted to succeed at the colliery, as it was positioned close to the houses of officials and skilled workers on Eakring Road.
--
Courtesy Inspire Picture Archive & Rex photographs

← Cross Street, Bilsthorpe, showing the village hall on the right. All of these buildings were commissioned by the Stanton Ironworks Company. The photograph was taken sometime between the late 1920s and early 30s.
--
Courtesy Inspire Picture Archive & Rex photographs

References

1. C. Hartwell, N. Pevsner, E, Williamson *The Buildings of England: Nottinghamshire* (Yale, 2020), p.132.

2. A. R. Griffin, *Mining in the East Midlands, 1550–1947* (Frank Cass, 1971), p.162–63.

↑ Layout plan of Bilsthorpe Housing Scheme, 1925 by Lambert & Trotter. Notice the allocation of staff houses for colliery officials in the bottom right corner along what is Eakring Road. The colours work as follows: yellow, Anglican church; red, nonconformist chapel; purple, pub; light blue, cinema; and dark blue, shops. This plan was later modified and reduced in scale, probably due to changes in the global demand for British coal which became apparent by this date.

--

Courtesy © Inspire Nottinghamshire Archives DC/SW/4/8/1/6

References

3. Nottinghamshire Archives, *Layout Plans of Bilsthorpe Housing Scheme*, DC/SW/4/8/1/1–2,4–5,8,11; Nottinghamshire Archives, *Plan of Block of two Type A Houses, Bilsthorpe Housing Scheme* DC/SW/4/8/1/3; Nottinghamshire Archives, *Block plan of Manager's House, Bilsthorpe*, DC/SW/4/8/1/9.

4. Historic OS mapping.

Housing

The layout and housing was designed by the architects A.E. Lambert and Anderson Trotter of Nottingham.[3] Lambert was already well regarded for his work in Nottingham, such as the Midland Station and Albert Hall (both Grade II listed). At Bilsthorpe Lambert and Trotter designed in the arts and crafts style with brick, roughcast render and occasional classical proportions. The first housing was laid out on a diagonal grid parallel with Eakring Road towards The Crescent to the rear.[4] The houses are generally arranged in short terraces of four units or as semi-detached blocks, as shown on the Ordnance Survey map revision of 1939. The houses are of brick, with some blocks completely or partially rendered. Front and rear gardens were provided. Archive plans suggest the houses were designed with three bedrooms with a front door leading to a small stair hall. The contractor was J. C. Short, who was advertising for bricklayers in 1925.

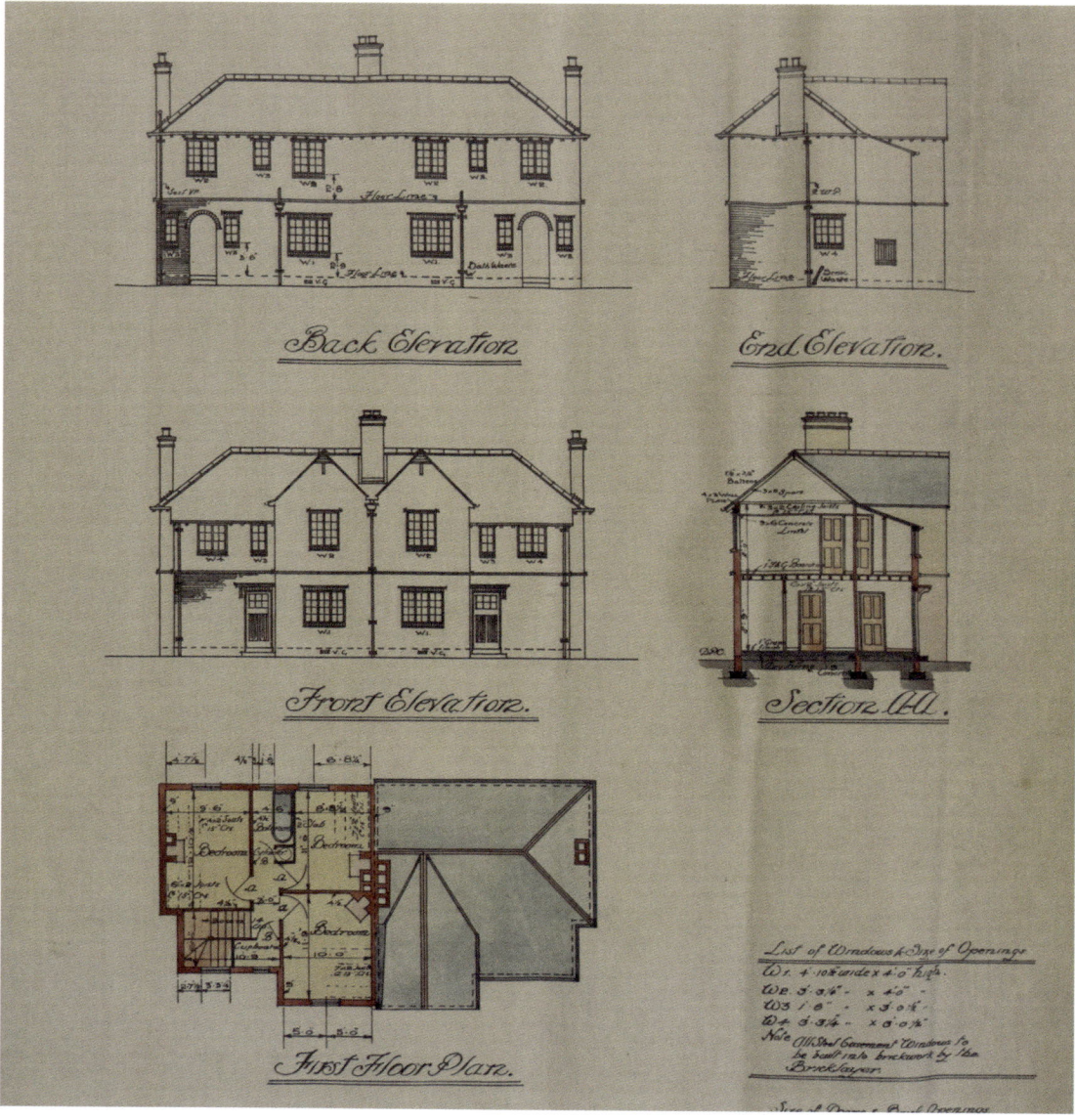

Back Elevation

End Elevation

Front Elevation

Section AA.

First Floor Plan.

List of Windows & Size of Openings

← Bilsthorpe Type B Houses, facing south, 1925. This type of house was built on Eakring Road and consisted of three bedrooms and a parlour. It was intended for officials and skilled workers. They were designed by the architects Lambert & Trotter of Nottingham.
--
Courtesy © Inspire Nottinghamshire Archives DC/SW/4/8/1/4

The management structure of the colliery company was neatly underpinned by the design of the estate. The colliery manager's house was positioned at a considerable distance from the estate but in view of the headstocks.[5] This can still be seen on Deerdale Lane and is a large detached house, named 'The Hill'. Officials and skilled workers were housed in semi-detached parlour housing on Eakring Road, nearest to the colliery entrance. Miners occupied the smaller non-parlour housing to the rear, each with 3 bedrooms and ground floor bathrooms. Houses along Savile Road were more spacious and desirable (some with hipped roofs) and positioned closest to Eakring Road.[6]

References

5. R. J. Waller, *The Dukeries Transformed: The Social and Political Development of a Twentieth Century Coalfield* (Clarendon Press, 1983), p.86.

6. Nottinghamshire Archives, *Layout plans of Bilsthorpe Housing Scheme*, DC/SW/4/8/1/1–2,4–5,8,11; Nottinghamshire Archives, *Plan of Block of two Type A Houses, Bilsthorpe Housing Scheme* DC/SW/4/8/1/3; Nottinghamshire Archives, *Block plan of Manager's House, Bilsthorpe*, DC/SW/4/8/1/9.

↓ Bilsthorpe Miners' Welfare, c.1958. The post-war nationalised coal industry could be more egalitarian than the old colliery companies.
--
Courtesy © Architectural Press Archive / RIBA Collections

↑ The Stanton Arms pub, Bilsthorpe. Originally built and managed by the Stanton Ironworks Company. Photograph taken 2021.
--
Courtesy © Chris Matthews

References

7. RIBA Architecture Image Library AP Box 784 1949–1963 (1) (H13233), Box 784 1949–1963 (1) (H13205).

8. R. J. Waller, T*he Dukeries Transformed: The Social and Political Development of a Twentieth Century Coalfield* (Clarendon Press, 1983), p.179–80.

9. Nottingham and Southwell Diocese church history project: http://southwellchurches.history.nottingham.ac.uk/

* hung tiles
the practice of installing tiles on vertical walls to funtion as a cladding

New building took place to the north of Mickledale Road from the 1950s, with brick built houses by the local district council. More expansion to the west of the original village followed with pre-fabricated concrete houses built by the National Coal Board. These were known as Cornish Type houses and designed by A. E. Beresford & R. Tonkin. Most of the Cornish Type 1 houses were later considered defective and have subsequently been reclad, though some of the distinctive mansard roofs have survived.

Amenities

A sports field, pavilion, village hall, and institute (since demolished) were provided by the colliery company. A miners' welfare institute was built to the designs of Michael Moss in Modernist style in 1958, on the site of the demolished St Luke's Church.[7] The design was considered noteworthy and a set of photographs of the newly completed building is held in the RIBA Architecture Image Library.

Memorials and Heritage

A winding wheel has been erected at the site of the colliery, and a mining heritage museum was opened near the village hall in 2014. Other memorials include a stone carving of a large miners' Davy lamp, inscribed with the names of those who had been killed at the colliery was unveiled in 2011. A statue of a miner was erected outside the pit but was later moved to the Bilsthorpe Heritage Museum. This commemorates the three miners who were killed in the disaster at Bilsthorpe Colliery in August 1993. Three mining union banners are also on display at the museum

Other Buildings

On The Crescent the Church of St Luke was a semi-permanent structure of timber and brick which was dedicated in 1932. It was initiated by the colliery company to counter the influence of the local rector at St Margaret's Church who was encouraging strike activity and membership of the Nottinghamshire Miners' Association. Its history though brief, is a neat example of how colliery companies could seek to try and depoliticise miners.[8] Nevertheless it was abandoned by 1939 and was later demolished.[9]

The Stanton Arms pub on Mickledale Lane seems to be part of the original layout and is shown on a map of 1939. This is an impressive brick arts and crafts building, with hung tiles,* decorated chimney stacks and roughcast render. The Crompton View School was built by the County Council to plans approved in 1926. The building is of brick in classical style, probably to designs by the County Architect's team. After the Second World War the County Council built Bilsthorpe Library using their prefabricated modernist CLASP system, finished with timber cladding. CLASP buildings were designed to be resilient to movement in mining areas. The essential component was a pin-jointed steel frame that could ride on a raft foundation with spring loaded cross bracing.

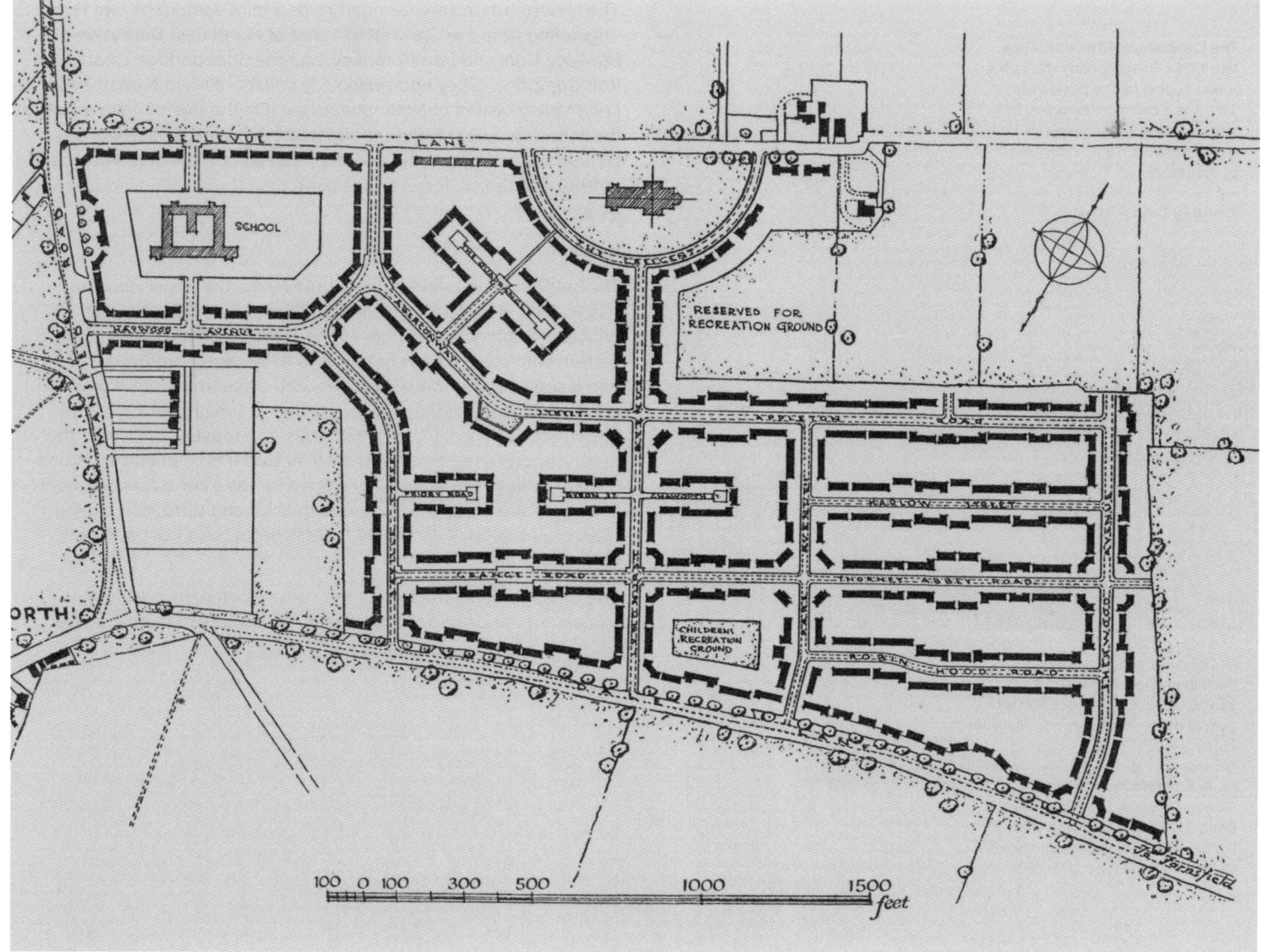

BLIDWORTH
Clare Hartwell & Chris Matthews

Company & Village

Blidworth is a small village with medieval origins.[1] Blidworth Colliery was sunk 1925-26 by the Newstead Colliery Company and was called Newstead No.2 until 1930. A colliery village was built by the Industrial Housing Association (IHA) between 1925–7 on a site to the north-east of the original settlement. The colliery was temporarily closed from 1930-32 to allow a new mining strategy to be introduced which involved installing better machinery.

↑ A 1920s plan for Blidworth colliery village by the Industrial Housing Association. With 838 new houses, Blidworth was one of the largest of the colliery villages developed during the inter-war period. Management housing was located east of Belle Vue Lane.

--

From J. T. Walters, *The Building of Twelve Thousand Houses* (Ernest Benn, 1927). Courtesy University of Nottingham Manuscripts and Special Collections, Oversize Em. G15 WAL

↓ The Quadrangle, Blidworth, circa late 1920s. Image clearly shows the round coping for the brick walls. This was a common feature of IHA villages. Photograph taken by John Henry Spree, a Nottinghamshire photographer.
--
Courtesy Dave Fordham

The Newstead Colliery Company was a joint venture by two firms originating from the Chesterfield area of North East Derbyshire; Staveley Coal and Iron Company, and the Sheepbridge Coal and & Iron Company.[2] They had previously collaborated at Newstead in the Leen Valley district of Nottinghamshire. On the eve of nationalisation the Staveley–Sheepbridge group had the greatest output of any colliery undertaking in the country.[3] The pit at Blidworth was closed in 1989 and the colliery site has been developed as an industrial estate.

Housing

The settlement was laid out and built by the Industrial Housing Association (IHA) for the colliery company on the Garden City principles common at that time. The layout is on a relaxed grid pattern with set-backs or green bays to break up the building line and a semi-circular road 'The Crescent' close to the colliery, which is the site of the mission hall. It was one of the largest projects undertaken by the IHA, with 838 houses.[4] Houses conform to the usual designs used by the IHA and include a type of corner house, used at street intersections, designed to add interest and variety to the street scene as well as semi-detached and terraced housing. Houses are of brick and some half-rendered with front and rear gardens.

The management structure of the colliery company clearly influenced the design of the estate. The colliery manager resided

→ Drawing of Belle Vue Lane and Mansfield Road, Blidworth. The Industrial Housing Association took care to design housing specifically for corner plots.
--
From J. T. Walters, *The Building of Twelve Thousand Houses* (Ernest Benn, 1927). Courtesy University of Nottingham Manuscripts and Special Collections, Oversize Em. G15 WAL

References

1. C. Hartwell, N. Pevsner, E, Williamson *The Buildings of England: Nottinghamshire* (Yale, 2020), p.137.

2. Durham Minig Museum Website, www.dmm.org.uk

3. A. R. Griffin, *Mining in the East Midlands, 1550–1947* (Frank Cass, 1971), p.163.

4. Hay & Fordham, *New Coalfields New Housing*, (Fedj-el-Adoum, 2017).

at 'Red House', on Belle Vue Lane, which is a large detached building near the colliery entrance and originally with spacious grounds.[5] Neighbouring this to the west, the head engineers and under managers were located at four large semi-detached parlour houses on Belle Vue Lane: The Villa, Inglewood, Westbury House and Pendenis.[6] To the rear, the most desirable houses for colliery deputies were generally located on The Crescent, while a mixture of house types was provided towards Dale Lane, most of which were designed with 3 bedrooms, scullery,* ground floor bathroom and living room.[7] By 1966 additional council housing south of Dale Road had been built and the settlement has since expanded with infill housing in areas such as The Crescent and recent developments between the old village and the colliery village.[8]

Amenities

Sports fields and allotments were provided as well as a miners' welfare institute. This is shown on a map of 1939 and possibly designed by George Warner in what was largely an arts and crafts design but with a beaux-arts plan and some neoclassical detailing. Since the closure of the colliery it has been demolished and replaced with a featureless Miners' Welfare Social Centre. St Andrew's Mission Hall was provided as an additional place of worship for the colliery community and for social events. The hall was dedicated in 1935 and built on land given by the colliery company. It was financed through the Diocesan Loan Fund, repaid through local fund raising. It is a modest Swedish style building with exterior red cladding and simple open roof structure.[9] A Primitive Methodist chapel was built on Dale Lane in traditional Gothic style in 1927–8. It has been converted for retail use.

The Forest Folk Inn was built by Home Brewery as a 'Trust Public House', to a design by the Nottinghamshire architect L. Dodsley which was subject to approval by the IHA architects. This scheme was devised to exercise control over designs and the brewery was expected to make contributions to community projects. The pub was named after James Prior's 1901 novel, *Forest Folk*, which was set in rural Blidworth. Following demolition in 2005 some of the stained glass on the theme of Sherwood Forest animals was saved and relocated to the mission hall.

A site for a school is shown on the IHA plan where it now stands and in 1924 a decision was taken by the County Council to provide a new school, now called Blidworth Oaks (originally named Blidworth County Council School and later Robert Jones). The building is of brick in simple classical style, probably to designs by the County Architect's team. After the Second World War Nottinghamshire County Council provided a library on New Lane, using the prefabricated modernist CLASP system with concrete panels and curtain wall glazing. On the edge of the village Mansfield Brewery built the Jolly Friar on Dale Lane in the 1960s. Amid its woodland backdrop it was designed in the style of a modernist lodge with hung tiles and a suitably jolly zig zag roof. This was recently demolished and replaced with new housing.

* scullery
a small kitchen or room used for washing dishes and household work

↓ Blidworth Welfare Institute, designed by George Warner and built at some point between 1925 and 1939. This photograph was taken in 1982 and the building has since been demolished.
--
Courtesy © Reg Baker & Picture Nottingham

References

5. Census Records & 1939 Register. See: findmypast.co.uk

6. Nottinghamshire Archives, *Blidworth Housing Scheme*, DC/SW/4/8/3/5, 7.

7. Nottinghamshire Archives, *Blidworth Housing Scheme*, DC/SW/4/8/3/5.

8. Historic OS mapping, local press reports.

9. Nottingham and Southwell Diocese church history project: http://southwellchurches.history.nottingham.ac.uk/

← Thoresby Colliery, 1939, the first all-electric coal mine in the country. This was at the request of Earl Manvers who wanted to minimise industrial smoke from his estate.

--

From: *Bolsover Jubilee Souvenir, 1889–1939*, (Bolsover Colliery Company, 1939). Courtesy University of Nottingham Manuscripts and Special Collections, Oversize Em. O46 BOL

EDWINSTOWE (THORESBY COLLIERY)
Chris Matthews

Company & Village

When Thoresby Colliery closed in 2015 it was the last remaining coal mine in Nottinghamshire, and one of the last deep mines operating in the UK, which was testament to its efficiency and productivity. It was also the last colliery founded by the Bolsover Colliery Company before the realities of falling global demand became apparent in the late 1920s. The initial plans were for a colliery village of 956 houses but only 497 were built.[1] Sinking began in 1925 and work could have begun sooner were it not for the reticence of the landowner Earl Manvers.[2] Manvers feared that country life at Edwinstowe would be compromised by the huge changes necessitated; mass housing, transport infrastructure and industrial plant. Nevertheless the potential earnings gained from coal royalties became too good to resist, so much in fact that it eventually became Manvers' main source of income. This revenue was brought to a close by the 1938 Coal Act when royalties were bought out by the government. Until then however, aristocrats such as Earl Manvers had an influence on how the industry should be conducted, but this was sometimes at odds with the power of the colliery companies.

To some degree the tension between the respective power of the aristocracy and the colliery companies was played out in the urban form of Thoresby model village at Edwinstowe. There was a genuine social divide in the village along the High Street; between the colliery company estate in the west; and the rural village in the east. Manvers succeeded in preventing a mineral railway line from running through the Birklands of Sherwood Forest in the north, and instead it had to arrive via a cutting beneath Ollerton Road in the east. Thoresby became the first all electric colliery in the country so that chimneys would not disfigure the Dukeries landscape. Unhappily for Earl Manvers however he was unable to completely prevent the visibility of smoke, or the naming of the colliery after his estate.[3]

References

1. R. J. Waller, *The Dukeries Transformed: The Social and Political Development of a Twentieth Century Coalfield* (Clarendon Press, 1983), pp.57–8.

2. R. J. Waller, *The Dukeries Transformed: The Social and Political Development of a Twentieth Century Coalfield* (Clarendon Press, 1983), pp.65–72.

3. R. J. Waller, *The Dukeries Transformed: The Social and Political Development of a Twentieth Century Coalfield* (Clarendon Press, 1983), pp.65–72.

← Edwinstowe Hall, c.1939. This was acquired by the Bolsover Colliery Company in 1923 and became the social headquarters for the firm. It was modified to accommodate a dining hall, games and conference rooms, dormitories, gymnasium and cinema.
--
From: *Bolsover Jubilee Souvenir, 1889–1939*, (Bolsover Colliery Company, 1939). Courtesy University of Nottingham Manuscripts and Special Collections, Oversize Em. O46 BOL

↓ Edwinstowe model village housing for miners. Similar in design to the Bolsover Colliery Company's earlier houses at Clipstone, although with more neoclassical details and restraint.
--
From: *Bolsover Jubilee Souvenir, 1889–1939*, (Bolsover Colliery Company, 1939). Courtesy University of Nottingham Manuscripts and Special Collections, Oversize Em. O46 BOL

Housing

Despite such tensions, in other instances there was a degree of harmony with the colliery companies, particularly in the paternalist approach to tied housing for its workers. In 1923 the agents for the Savile and Manvers estates agreed that the new colliery villages should not encroach on their country seats: Ollerton was to remain east of the Maun, while Edwinstowe was developed no further south than the railway line.[4] Manvers also sold a number of buildings to the colliery company, which in some ways perpetuated the culture of deference to the squirearchy. Perhaps the most telling example were the Georgian country homes acquired by the Bolsover Colliery Company. Edwinstowe Hall became a Welfare Centre in 1923, while the Managing Director of the company, T. E. B. Young, resided at Edwinstowe House.[5] Young was later knighted and became Production Member to the National Coal Board.[6]

The Bolsover Company built new housing for management, which was positioned east of the model village and close to the colliery entrance on Ollerton Road. The manager Charles Edward Woodward lived in a large detached house called Edwinstowe Lodge,[7] though this was later demolished in the post-war period to make way for the Maid Marion Drive estate. Nearby at The Villas (1–4 Ollerton Road), the Chief Clerk, Head Electrician and Head Engineer lived in spacious semi-detached accommodation of two types. The pair nearest the colliery was the largest with 4 bed, drawing room,

References

4. R. J. Waller, *The Dukeries Transformed: The Social and Political Development of a Twentieth Century Coalfield* (Clarendon Press, 1983), p.68.

5. R. J. Waller, *The Dukeries Transformed: The Social and Political Development of a Twentieth Century Coalfield* (Clarendon Press, 1983), p.85.

6. B. Supple, *The History of the British Coal Industry, Volume 4, 1913–46: The Political Economy of Decline* (Clarendon Press, 1987), p.673.

7. R. J. Waller, *The Dukeries Transformed: The Social and Political Development of a Twentieth Century Coalfield* (Clarendon Press, 1983), p.85.

References

8. 1939 Register. See: findmypast.co.uk; Nottinghamshire Archives, *Plan of proposed semi-detached dwellings* DC/SW/4/8/9/3.

9. Edwinstowe Historical Society, *Housing: Bolsover Colliery Company Edwinstowe Housing Plans*, see: https://edwinstowehistory.org.uk/local-history/buildings/housing/

10. M. Woodhead, *Edwinstowe – The Coming of Coal* (Edwinstowe Historical Society, 2010), pp.11–17.

11. R. J. Waller, *The Dukeries Transformed: The Social and Political Development of a Twentieth Century Coalfield* (Clarendon Press, 1983), p.83.

↓ Plan of proposed semi-detached dwellings to be built at Edwinstowe for the Bolsover Colliery Co Ltd, Chesterfield, 1925. These were intended for colliery officials and known as 'The Villas'. They can still be seen at 1–4 Ollerton Road.
--
Courtesy Inspire Nottinghamshire Archives, DC/SW/4/8/9/3

* fenestration
the arrangement of windows and openings in a building.

dining room, kitchen, attic room and bay window. The type nearest the village was smaller and with no attic room or bay window.[8] The rectilinear plan form of the model village was also very similar to that at Clipstone, with occasional crescents and cul-de-sacs setback from linear routes. However, probably owing to a relatively elongated plot, Edwinstowe was designed without an oval circus at the centre.

Original plans for the housing from 1928 show that the architectural practice responsible was Percy B Houfton of Chesterfield. However, Houfton had died in 1926, so it is likely that work was conducted by his former colleagues. Like Houfton's earlier designs (Bolsover, Rainworth and Clipstone), Edwinstowe was built with an egalitarian mixture of house types throughout the estate, with five types each of parlour and non-parlour houses, in order to accommodate corner plots, semi-detached and groups of three or four.[9] Building work was conducted in three phases 1926–31 and the bricks were supplied by the Bolsover Colliery Company's own brickworks in Derbyshire. All houses were designed with three bedrooms, bathroom, toilet, living room, scullery, larder, cooking range, back boiler and coal house.[10] Oral history accounts show that there was preference among overmen for First Avenue, while Fifth Avenue was considered least desirable.[11] Architecturally, the houses share many similarities with Clipstone and Rainworth, such as the fenestration* and entrance entablature, but overall the approach was a little cleaner with no pantiles or facing gables.

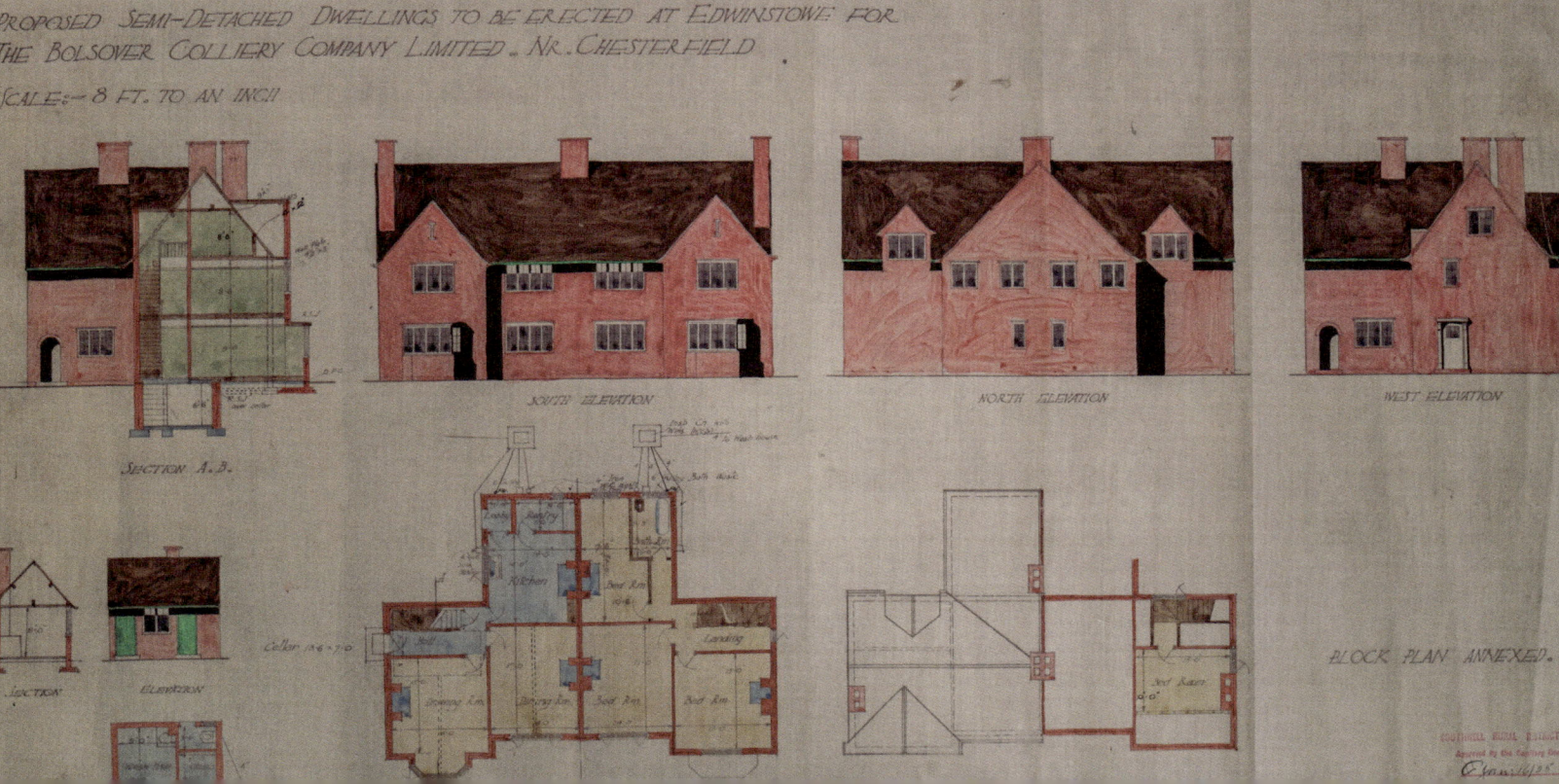

← Sports pavilion, Edwinstowe. This is located at the western end of Fourth Avenue, at what is now Thoresby Football Club and Cricket Club. The front of the building has since been modified.

--

From: *Bolsover Jubilee Souvenir, 1889–1939*, (Bolsover Colliery Company, 1939). Courtesy University of Nottingham Manuscripts and Special Collections, Oversize Em. O46 BOL

Amenities

By 1931 the village had grown to a population of 2,818 people and this necessitated a wide variety of amenities. The earliest and best surviving amenity building is the Gymnasium which was built next to Edwinstowe Hall and designed in 1923. It featured a hall, office, classroom, balcony, stores, concrete ceiling and ventilator.[12] A Bolsover Colliery Co plaque in the central pediment can still be seen from Church Street. By 1932 the bowling and putting green had been laid out and this was followed by a pavilion and sports ground opened four years later. Until an adequate Miners' Institute was built, accommodation was found in 'The Club', which is now a clinic on Fourth Avenue. The Thoresby Miners' Institute was built in 1939 by Bolsover Colliery Co in a muted Art Deco/Dudok style, but was demolished in 1996 and replaced with a nursing home.[13] On the opposite side of the central square; the Welfare Hall has also been demolished. This was built in 1932–3 by the Thoresby Miners' Welfare Committee, and designed by the architects Cursk, Howard and Lane of Mansfield.[14] Plans show it contained a kitchen, small hall, main hall, stage, dressing room and billiards room.[15] Similarly the Major Cinema on Mansfield Road (built 1936), and the original 1924 King Edwin School have also been demolished. This was designed in a simple classical style by the County architects department.

Later Developments

After the Second World War the village was extended with council housing to the west and a new privately built estate in the north. Nottinghamshire County Council provided a new library on the High Street, using the prefabricated modernist CLASP system, originally with timber panels. The village was provided with pubs before the arrival of the colliery company, but since the 1920s changes in the local population encouraged the upgrading of existing venues during the inter-war period, such as the Royal Oak and Robin Hood Inn. The Manvers Arms on Welbeck Drive was the only entirely new pub built in the post-war period, this was designed in the Scandinavian modernist style with generous ground floor windows. It was demolished in very recent years and replaced with modernist bungalows.

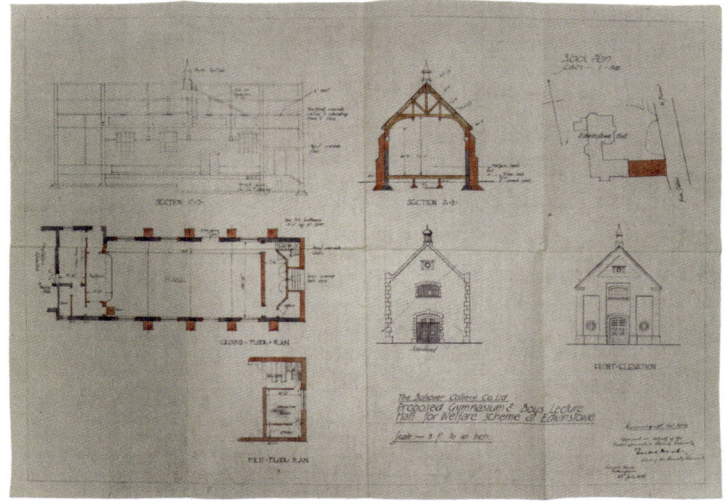

↑ Proposed gymnasium and boys lecture hall by the Bolsover Colliery Company, 1923. This building still stands on Church Street.

--

Courtesy Inspire Nottinghamshire Archives CC/CL/2/5/2/46

References

12. Nottinghamshire Archives CC/CL/2/5/2/46

13. Edwinstowe Historical Society, *Thoresby Miners' Institute*, see: https://edwinstowehistory.org.uk/local-history/organisations/thoresby-miners-institute/

14. Edwinstowe Historical Society, *Welfare Hall*, https://edwinstowehistory.org.uk/local-history/buildings/welfare-hall/

15. Nottinghamshire Archives, *Plan of new village hall*, DC/SW/4/8/9/14.

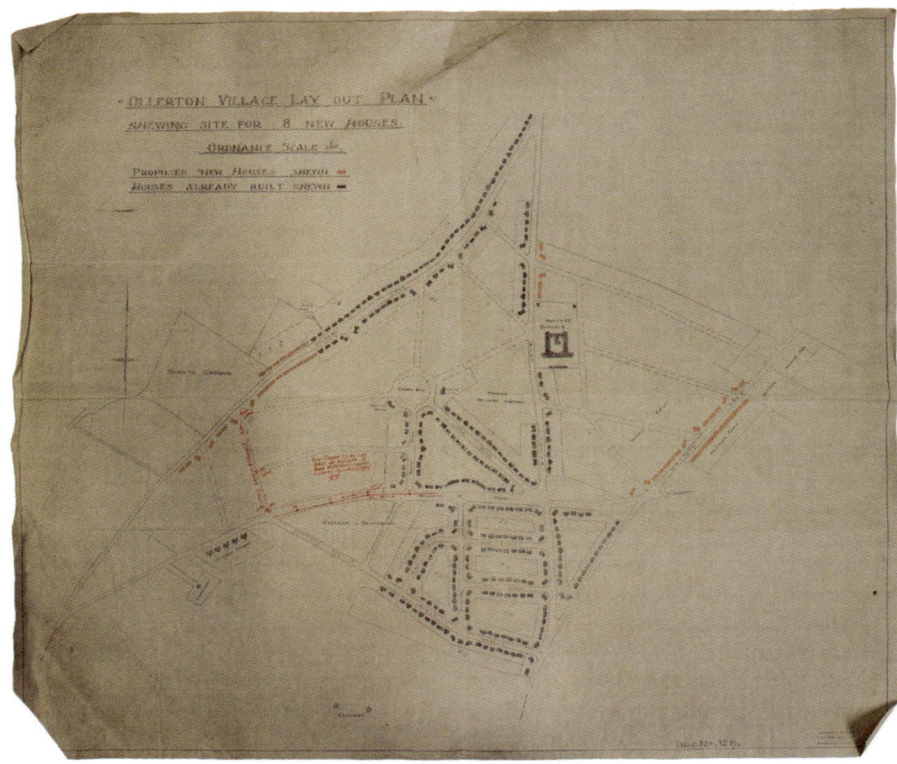

→ Ollerton village layout plan, showing
site for proposed new houses, 1929.
The site for the church is positioned a
the centre, the local authority school
to the right and housing for officials
towards the left-hand corner.
--
Courtesy Inspire Nottinghamshire
Archives, DC/SW/4/8/20/26

References

1. A. R. Griffin, *Mining in the East
    Midlands, 1550–1947* (Frank Cass, 1971),
    pp.24–25

2. A. R. Griffin, *Mining in the East
    Midlands, 1550–1947* (Frank Cass, 1971),
    p.106. In its early years 1790–1810
    the Butterley Company was called
    Benjamin Outram and Company.

3. R. J. Waller, *The Dukeries Transformed:
    The Social and Political Development
    of a Twentieth Century Coalfield*
    (Clarendon Press, 1983), p.14; A. R.
    Griffen, *The British Coalmining Industry:
    Retrospect & Prospect* (1977), p.167.

NEW OLLERTON
Chris Matthews

Company & Village

The Butterley Company was one of the most prestigious businesses
operating in the region. It was at the heart of the industrial revolution
in the East Midlands, instigating the turnpikes, canals and railways,
and its ironwork was nationally sought after, most famously for the
roof span of St Pancras Station in London.[1] Butterley was established
as a joint stock enterprise in 1790 to work the iron and coal reserves
of the exposed coalfield near Ripley in Derbyshire. The undertaking
was successful, not least because it could ensure a steady demand
for coal via its ironworks.[1] Its founders were expert in their respective
fields: Benjamin Outram, a canal and railway engineer; William
Jessop, nationally renowned civil engineer; and John Wright, a
successful Nottingham banker. By 1890 the firm was moving into
the concealed coalfield with Kirkby Colliery in Nottinghamshire,
which was one of the biggest collieries in the country and provided
housing with bathrooms for employees.[2] Further expansion was
initiated in 1917 when Butterley went into a joint coal proving
venture (demonstrating the viability of coal reserves) with the
Stanton Ironworks Company at Ollerton and agreed a lease with the
landholder Lord Savile. Eventually Stanton pulled out of the project
and Butterley bought out their half share.[3]

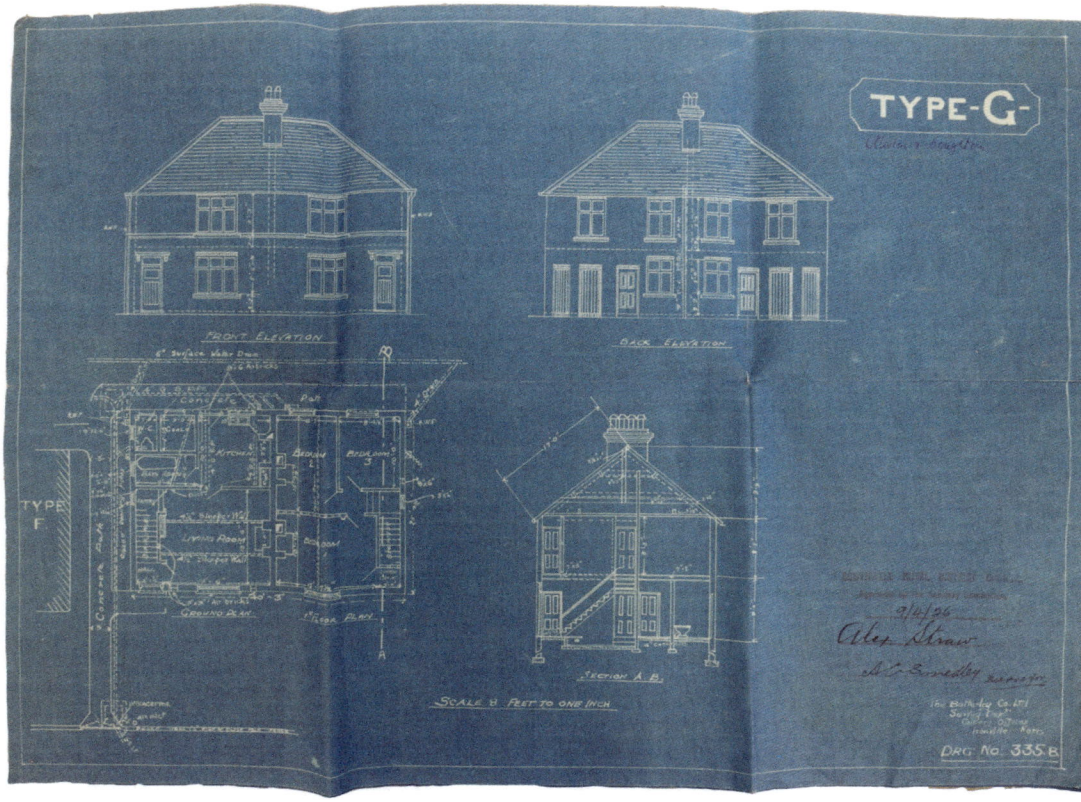

← Plans showing a Type G house to be erected at Ollerton, 1926. With only a ground floor living room and no parlour, this house type would have been among the most affordable. Also notice the ground floor bathroom: having this positioned near the rear entrance would have helped to prevent the spread of coal dust to the living room and bedrooms .
--
Courtesy Inspire Nottinghamshire Archives, DC/SW/4/8/20/16

New Ollerton became one of the largest model villages in the Dukeries with approximately 932 houses by the Second World War. This was second only to Harworth Colliery with 1,100 houses at the very north of the county.[4] Harworth was developed by Barber, Walker & Company, who had famously collaborated with Butterley in the early development of the Midland Railway.[5] The housing at New Ollerton is very similar to Butterley's accommodation at Kirkby in Ashfield and was built by a company from the same town, Messrs Coleman and Blackburn.[6] However, in terms of scale, planning and amenities, New Ollerton was far greater, partly owing to its relatively isolated position. Like Edwinstowe there was often a conflict of attitudes between miners and rural villagers who had experienced great changes in local retail, rent and employment.[7] This was intensified by the speed and scale of the change: Ollerton Colliery was sunk between 1923–25 and by 1932 the company had built 832 houses increasing the total population to 3912. The village had grown fivefold in the space of ten years.[8] However, compared to Edwinstowe this conflict was mitigated by the relative distance of the new model village from Old Ollerton. For example, the new church of St Paulinus. was nearly a mile to the north-east of the medieval St Giles.

References

4. R. J. Waller, *The Dukeries Transformed: The Social and Political Development of a Twentieth Century Coalfield* (Clarendon Press, 1983), p.79.

5. Lenton Times, *The Campus: Facing up to its Past*, Issue 4, June 1990.

6. R. J. Waller, *The Dukeries Transformed: The Social and Political Development of a Twentieth Century Coalfield* (Clarendon Press, 1983), p.77.

7. R. J. Waller, *The Dukeries Transformed: The Social and Political Development of a Twentieth Century Coalfield* (Clarendon Press, 1983), pp.62–64.

8. R. J. Waller, *The Dukeries Transformed: The Social and Political Development of a Twentieth Century Coalfield* (Clarendon Press, 1983), p.27.

References

9. C. Hartwell, N. Pevsner, E, Williamson *The Buildings of England: Nottinghamshire* (Yale, 2020), p.534.

10. R. J. Waller, *The Dukeries Transformed: The Social and Political Development of a Twentieth Century Coalfield* (Clarendon Press, 1983), pp.84–5.

11. 1939 Register. See: findmypast.co.uk

12. Nottinghamshire Archives, *New Ollerton Colliery Plan Showing Proposed Village*, MP/OL/1/1–2/R; Nottinghamshire Archives, Plan Showing Two Streets Proposed to be made at Ollerton for the Butterley Company Ltd,DC/SW/4/8/20/6.

* recessed elevations
walls set back from the main building to create variation

↓ Miners' housing, Forest Road, Ollerton, c.1930s,
--
Courtesy © Picture Nottingham

Housing

In some respects this distance between Old and New Ollerton was used to the advantage of the colliery company when planning their model village. At the top of the village hierarchy was Ollerton Hall, a Georgian mansion located close to the centre of the old village.[9] This was rented from Lord Savile to provide accommodation for the colliery manger Montague Wright and served to perpetuate a tradition of aristocratic deference and paternalism.[10] East along Forest Road, the colliery village began with 3 pairs of large semi-detached parlour houses known as Savile Row. These were earmarked for second tier management; under mangers, clerks, surveyors and deputies.[11] Further east between 1 and 44 Forest Road, officials and skilled miners were accommodated in similar though slightly smaller houses. The miners' accommodation was positioned in the eastern most part of the village, all of which was semi-detached housing with variation created through a diversity of house types influenced by the style of the arts and crafts movement; recessed elevations,* hipped roofs and facing gables. Most were designed with 3 bedrooms, with ground floor living room, kitchen and water closet. The layout largely follows the ideals of the garden city movement, with a strong radial route around St Paulinus church and Briar Road forming a central axis. Building plans show that design work was carried out by either an unnamed architect or the survey department of the Butterley Company.[12]

↑ Savile Row, Forest Road: three pairs of semi-detached houses for management, built by the Butterley Company.
--
Courtesy © Chris Matthews

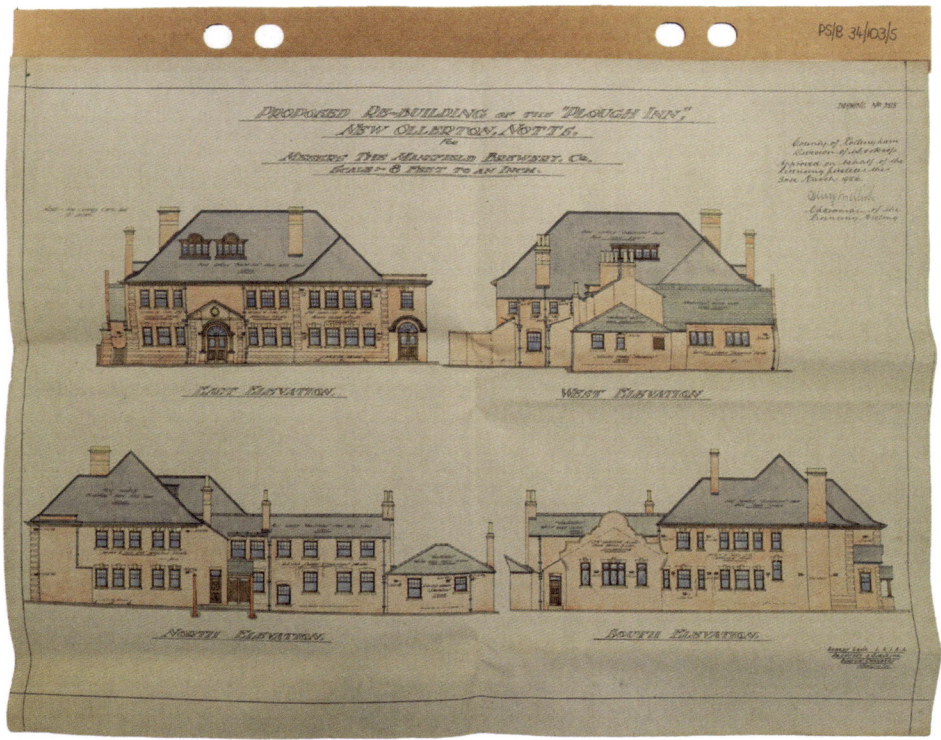

PS/B 34/103/5

← Plans for the rebuilding of the Plough Inn at New Ollerton, by Aubrey Lane, for Mansfield Brewery, March 1926. This large building was intended to accommodate temporary mining contractors and social events. These plans show designs for a lounge, serving bar, billiard room, kitchen, vaults, snug, smoking room and five bedrooms.
--
Courtesy Inspire Nottinghamshire Archives, C/PS/B/34/103

Amenities

The model village at Ollerton was well provided with amenities. Originally pithead baths were seen as unnecessary because water was heated at the colliery and circulated to miners' homes via external pipes. In the late 1920s the Miners' Welfare Committee gave £5,000 for a new Miners' Institute.[13] This was built in 1928 along Whinney Lane to a rather plain design. A modernist building was established in the post-war period. In recent years both structures have been demolished and replaced with housing. Uniquely for the Dukeries the Butterley Company built a hosiery factory in 1937 to employ miners' wives. This was leased to Hall and Earl of Leicester and located south of the railway line along Newark Road. It was demolished in the early 2000s.

Like Clipstone and Blidworth the shopping district is the only irregularly laid out area from the inter-war period. Here, the colliery company leased plots of land for retail developments, which prospective traders developed. At Ollerton these were located on the southern side of the Forest Road junction with Sherwood Drive, which in the Butterley plans was earmarked for the builders Coleman and Blackburn.[14] The most striking structure was the neo-classical Picture House, which was built in 1928 and demolished in the 2010s.[15] The Butterley Company did not allow pubs near the village centre; The Plough Inn was built in 1926 and positioned as far west as possible. This building was designed by Aubrey Lane for

← The impressive neoclassical detailing of the Plough Inn.
--
Courtesy © Chris Matthews

References

13. R. J. Waller, *The Dukeries Transformed: The Social and Political Development of a Twentieth Century Coalfield* (Clarendon Press, 1983), p.93; Nottinghamshire Archives, *Block plan of Whinney Lane, Ollerton, showing site of Miners' Welfare, 1929*, DC/SW/4/8/20/28.

14. Nottinghamshire Archives, *New Ollerton Colliery Plan Showing Proposed Village*, MP/OL/1/1–2/R.

15. Nottinghamshire Archives, *Plan of Proposed Cinema: Ollerton*, CC/CL/2/5/4/2 1925.

St Paulinus Church, Ollerton, dedicated to a seventh century Roman missionary who baptised converts in the River Trent.
--
Courtesy Inspire Picture Archive & Antoine collection

↑ The interior of St Paulinus, notice the quality of the brickwork. The church was Grade II listed in 1986
--
Courtesy © Chris Matthews

the Mansfield Brewery in the neoclassical Queen Anne style.[16] It is impressive in scale and architectural ambition; originally featuring a snug, smoke room, vaults, lounge hall, billiard room, club room and five bedrooms.

The most notable surviving public building from the original colliery village is the Church of St Paulinus. This was billed as 'the cathedral of the new coalfield' by the Butterley Company and is located at the very centre of the model village plan. Originally the company employed the nationally renowned architect Sir Giles Gilbert Scott in 1926 but later dismissed him. Subsequently they appointed Naylor, Sale and Woore of Derby and the church was consecrated in 1932. It is built in the Romanesque style and listed at Grade II.[17] To the west of the church stood the doctor's house and to the east the curates. Both of which were relatively large detached buildings.[18] Nottinghamshire County Council built a new school on Whinney Lane in a brick classical style. Building works were delayed by Southwell Rural District Council, who was struggling to complete the sewerage system on time. The building eventually opened in 1927.[19]

Later Developments

After the Second World War the village was gradually extended to the north, east and west, with a mixture of local authority and privately built housing. This expansion was considerable and probably necessitated by the development of Bevercotes colliery, which started production in 1958 (later delayed by geological problems and restarted 1971/72). The County Council provided a new school complex off Whinney Lane in 1964 using their prefabricated modernist CLASP building system. This was similar to Ollerton Library on Forest Road, finished using hung tiles, panelling and large areas of glazing. Since the closure of the colliery in 1994 there have been substantial regeneration projects. A business park named Sherwood Energy Village has been established on the site of the coal mine. It is now home to Centre Parcs Head Office, Experian, county council offices and a variety of other businesses.

Memorials

There are two mining memorials which are both positioned near the former entrance to the colliery on what is now Edison Rise. The earliest is a simple steel bench beside the entrance to the Asda supermarket. This pays tribute to the striking Yorkshire miner David Gareth Jones, who died while picketing at Ollerton Colliery in 1984. On the opposite side of the road is a statue of a miner commemorating the workers of Ollerton Colliery by the steel fabricator Ray Londale. It was commissioned by The Colliery Memorial Working Party in 2019. The Ollerton NUM banner, lost during the 1984-85 Miners' Strike, was later found in Southampton and returned. It has since been restored and now is on display above the west entrance of St Paulinus Church.

References

16. Nottinghamshire Archives, C/PS/B/34/103, *Rebuilding of the 'Plough Inn'*, 1926.

17. R. J. Waller, *The Dukeries Transformed: The Social and Political Development of a Twentieth Century Coalfield* (Clarendon Press, 1983), p.91.

18 Nottinghamshire Archives, *Various New Ollerton Colliery Village plans*, DC/SW/4/8/20/2.

19. R. J. Waller, *The Dukeries Transformed: The Social and Political Development of a Twentieth Century Coalfield* (Clarendon Press, 1983), p.167.

← Calverton colliery was an excellent modernist complex which was planned by Geoffrey Jellicoe with the architects branch of the Miners' Welfare Commission. They later designed the pithead baths in conformity with the whole scheme. Image shows the pithead baths as seen from the office block. Unfortunately the entire complex was demolished following the closure of the colliery in 1999.
--
From 'Calverton Colliery, Nottinghamshire', in *The Architect and Building News, 10th May 1940, pp.114–119.*

CALVERTON

Clare Hartwell & Chris Matthews

Background

Calverton was a small village with medieval origins which developed an economy based on agriculture and hosiery manufacture. The investment in a new colliery at Calverton signified both the increasing trend towards amalgamation during the inter-war period and the increasing shift of major new British coal mining activity towards Nottinghamshire.[1] Calverton heralded the central importance of the East Midlands for productivity and profitability.[2]

B. A. Collieries sank the first Calverton shaft in 1937 to reach the Bestwood Top Hard seam reserves. Once it was completed miners travelled in buses from Bestwood to the Calverton shaft to reduce underground travel and improve coal face working time. This arrangement lasted until 1948 when the Bestwood seams were exhausted and Calverton became a colliery in its own right. Following nationalisation in 1947, Calverton was developed as an independent colliery by the NCB and opened in 1952. The first shaft was completed in 1939 and used as a satellite shaft for Bestwood Colliery. Colliery buildings were erected at Calverton and a settlement started to the north-west of the old village.

After the war, work resumed and a second shaft was commenced in 1946. This was the first pit to be opened by the National Coal Board following nationalisation in 1947. The colliery was planned to produce one million tons of coal a year for 100 years. The mine closed in 1999, the colliery buildings were demolished and the site repurposed.

↑ Senior miners' housing on North Green, Calverton. Designed by Geoffrey Jellicoe and built in the late 1930s for B.A. Colleries Ltd.
--
Courtesy © Chris Matthews

References

1. B. Supple, *The History of the British Coal Industry, Volume 4, 1913–46: The Political Economy of Decline* (Clarendon Press, 1987), pp.201–9.

2. B. Supple, *The History of the British Coal Industry, Volume 4, 1913–46: The Political Economy of Decline* (Clarendon Press, 1987), p.672.

3. C. Hartwell, N. Pevsner, E, Williamson *The Buildings of England: Nottinghamshire* (Yale, 2020), p.161

4. 'Calverton Colliery, Nottinghamshire', in *The Architect and Building News*, 10th May 1940, pp.114–119.

5. Historic OS mapping, local press reports.

Housing

The designer of the colliery layout and village was Geoffrey Jellicoe, one of the most accomplished British landscape architects of the twentieth century. His designs were produced in collaboration with the architects' branch of the Miners' Welfare Commission and work was undertaken by Richard Wilson of the Jellicoe practice.[3] The plans, photographs and an account of the colliery buildings and village were published in 1940, by which time only small numbers of the proposed 500 homes had been completed and building had ceased due to war time conditions.[4] Houses were designed in a clean arts and craft style, with pleasing proportions, pantiles, entrance entablature and dormer windows. They were plotted at varied distances from the road to avoid the feeling of 'a continuous street' and brick walls were originally whitewashed to contrast with the working life of the colliery. Most of these homes survive, such as the 18 semi-detached houses on North Green, opposite the colliery site, which were intended for senior miners, while the 4 houses on Hollywood Lane are slightly larger and presumably for under managers and overmen. The colliery manager's house on Bartley Gardens has since been demolished and replaced with a small housing estate.

Work resumed in 1946, but it appears that Jellicoe's plan for housing remained largely unrealised. Large new housing schemes were instead undertaken during the 1950s by Basford Rural District Council and by the National Coal Board. The housing included prefab homes and concrete cottages. Most have been rebuilt or re-clad but quite a number can be found in the Labray Road area.[5] Such as the Central Cornwall Concrete & Artificial Stone Co. 'Type 1' houses (with steep mansard roofs*) and 'Type 2' (with conventional roofs).

Amenities& Memorials

Sports fields were laid out and a Miners' Welfare social club on Hollinwood Lane built in 1963. This has been rebuilt in recent years and is now known as The Top Club – Calverton Miners' Welfare. A winding wheel has been erected at what was the colliery entrance on Hollinwood Lane. A restored mine car erected in 2010 stands on Mansfield Road.

Later Developments

The village expanded with provision of a shopping centre, leisure facilities, library and schools during the post-war period. Some of these public buildings were built by Nottinghamshire County Council using their prefabricated modernist CLASP system. Perhaps most notable was the Sir John Sherbrooke Primary School which featured an impressive mural based on medieval carvings from the local parish church.

* mansard roof
a type of roof having two slopes on every side, the lower slope being considerably steeper

↑ A precast concrete Cornish Type 2 house on Flats Lane, Calverton. One of many commissioned by the National Coal Board, c.1946–1960.
--
Courtesy © Chris Matthews

↑ Calverton mine car, Mansfield Road: a memorial to the colliery.
--
Courtesy © Chris Matthews

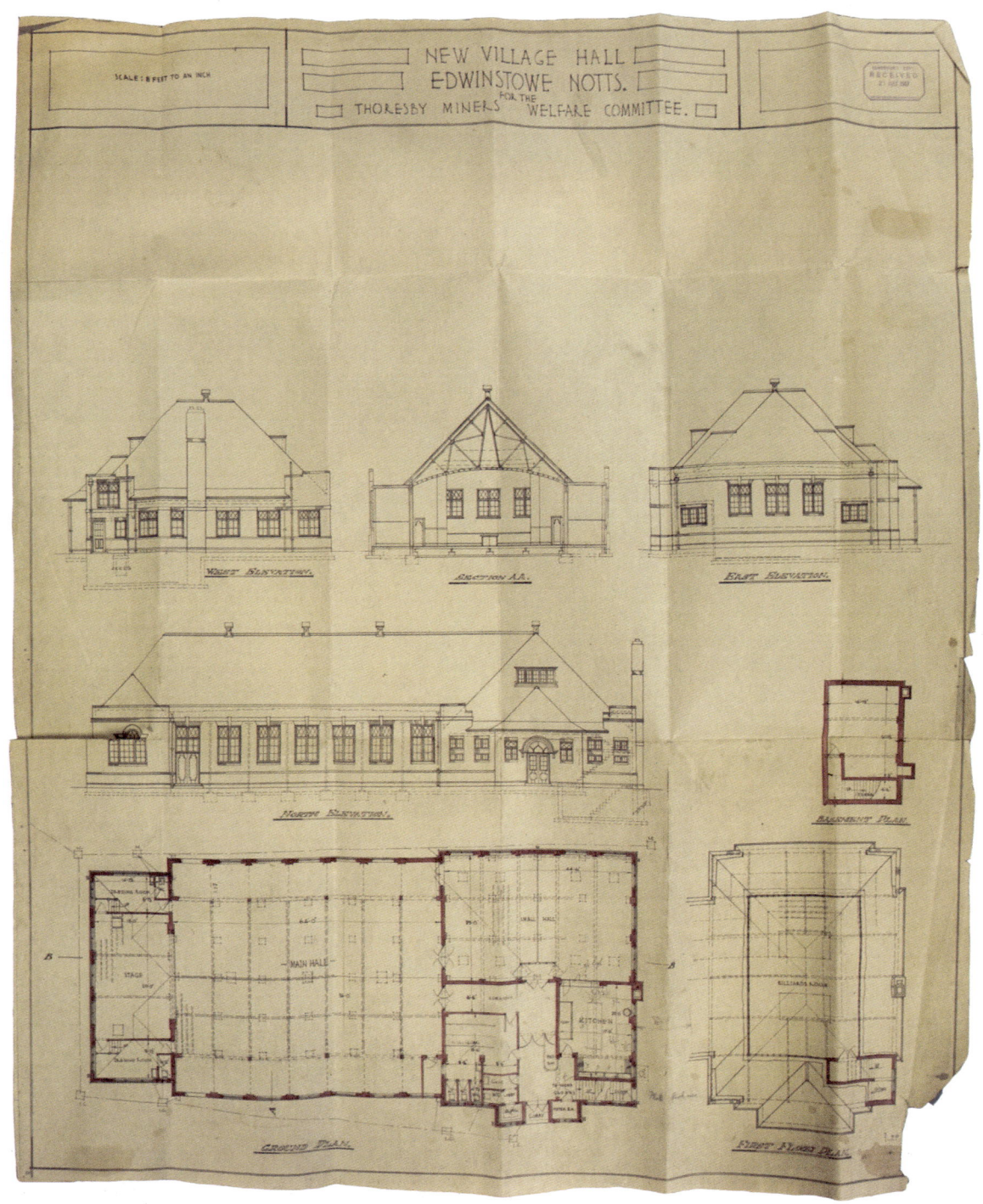

SCALE: 8 FEET TO AN INCH

NEW VILLAGE HALL
EDWINSTOWE NOTTS.
FOR THE
THORESBY MINERS WELFARE COMMITTEE.

WEST ELEVATION.

SECTION AA.

EAST ELEVATION.

NORTH ELEVATION.

BASEMENT PLAN.

GROUND PLAN.

FIRST FLOOR PLAN.

CONCLUSION
The historical legacy of the Nottinghamshire coalfield

References

1. D. Edgerton, *The Rise & Fall of the British Nation: A Twentieth Century History* (Penguin, 2018), pp.10–19, 83, & 385–94

2. A. R. Griffin, *The British Coal Mining Industry* (Moorland, 1977), pp.169–174.

3. C. Matthews, *Homes & Places: A History of Nottingham's Council Housing* (Nottingham City Homes, 2nd Edition, 2018), pp.114 & 117–118.

4. *Bolsover Jubilee Souvenir, 1889–1939* (Bolsover Colliery Company Ltd, 1939).

5. J. T. Walters, *The Building of Twelve Thousand Houses* (Ernest Benn, 1927).

There is a great deal of historical debate concerning the causes of British industrial decline. The aristocracy, the professional class and trade unions have all been blamed in one form or another. However, a more convincing picture concerns the nature of the British economy and its relationship with a changing world.[1] In light of which, the coal industry is an excellent example. Early British success in this field was predicated on easily accessible coal and weak competition. These advantages crumbled after the First World War as coal became harder to access and other nations found new sources of energy.[2] Unwittingly the Dukeries was developed at this tipping point; by 1925 there was a clear imbalance in profitability in comparison with other coalfields. The stories of industrial disputes and breakaway unions highlight this strain in British economic development. This was a country struggling to reconcile its early success with its future ambitions. It was a shame this situation could not have been managed smoothly.

Coal mines were never built to last but the villages have stood the test of time. One lesson from these places is the profitability of good housing. Today many people spend a lot of effort in trying to convince government to invest in good housing.[3] The basic argument is that healthy housing improves employability, which in turn increases tax revenue. It is remarkable therefore that a similar calculation was made by the colliery companies of the East Midlands. Expenditure on housing was vital for ensuring a regular supply of labour and a return on the initial investment. The Bolsover Colliery Company was responsible for six model villages with a combined population of 40,000.[4] The Industrial Housing Association built 12,000 houses during the 1920s.[5] It was as prolific as a city council. Using history to remedy present day problems always comes with a caveat: the past was a different place. In this age of mass communication and individualism many of the social controls practiced by the colliery companies would be neither desirable nor functional.

Of course these views don't have to be taken to heart, there are countless other perspectives on the history of the British coal industry but what can't be ignored so easily are the bricks and mortar of the colliery villages. What can we make of these places?

← Plans for a welfare hall at Edinwstowe, c.1932. It was commissioned by Thoresby Miners' Welfare Committee and designed by the architects Cursk, Howard and Lane of Mansfield. The building featured a main hall, stage, dressing rooms, small hall, kitchen and billiards room. It has since been demolished.
--
Courtesy Inspire Nottinghamshire Archives DC/SW/4/8/9/14

At first glance the Nottinghamshire coalfield villages are no different from any other industrial British town that was developed between the late nineteenth and early twentieth century; rows of red brick terraces, gradually giving way to garden city estates. Yet on closer inspection there are some telling characteristics: their often rural location, the urban hierarchy of the company, their paternalist amenities and stylistic preferences. No two model villages are the same. Bestwood is easily the most attractive of the nineteenth century colliery developments in Nottinghamshire. The most varied designs of the inter-war years belonged to those villages built by the Industrial Housing Association, such as Newstead, Blidworth and Warsop Vale. The Bolsover villages were solid and spacious, while Stanton at Bilsthorpe was tightly organised. If only B.A. Collieries had completed the initial plan at Calverton and the colliery buildings had been repurposed. The Jellicoe housing that was built here presents a refreshingly modern approach on the eve of nationalisation.

It is hoped that this study will shed new light on this district for the purposes of heritage and historic building conservation. More work could have been undertaken on the social and cultural experience of these places. Local historical studies by Pauline Marples and Margaret Woodhead provide a fitting example.[6] But it is healthy to leave material for other people to exploit and create new perspectives. History is a very gradual and collective experience, though also one which requires individual study. The history of the Nottinghamshire colliery villages is without doubt significant: it is rich in material for questioning the social and economic development of the country.

References

6. P. Marples, *Forest Town: The Village that Grew out of Coal* (Forest Town Heritage Group, 2005); M. Woodhead, *Edwinstowe – The Coming of Coal* (Edwinstowe Historical Society, 2010).

← The Venue, Rainworth, 2021. This was originally the Picture House cinema and could house 400 people. It was built in 1920 and has been substantially altered since.
--
Courtesy © Chris Matthews

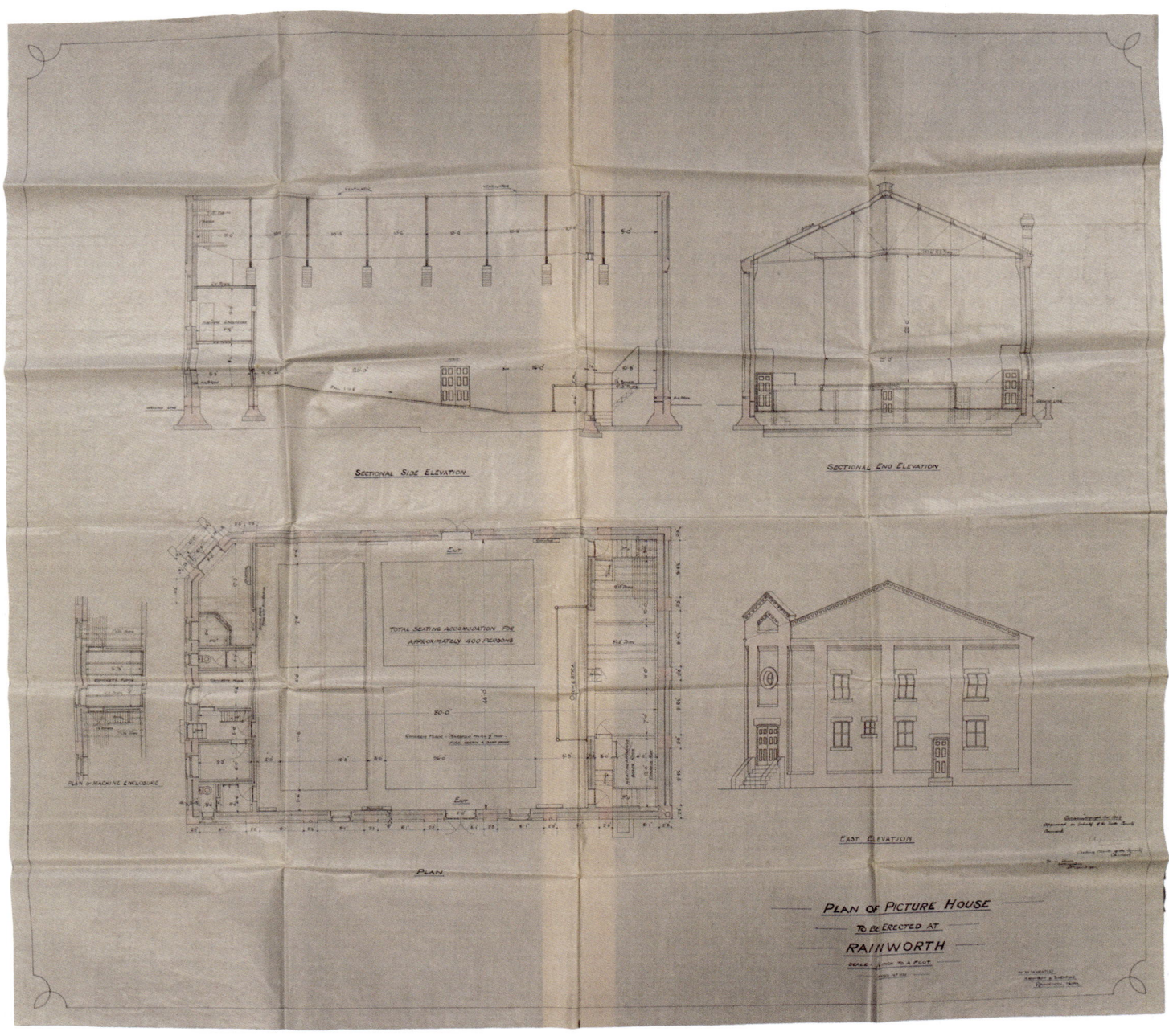

Original 1920 plan for Rainworth
Picture House by W. W. Wheatley.
It is interesting to compare this design
with the photograph on the left.

--

Courtesy © Inspire Nottinghamshire
Archives CC/CL/2/5/2/40

ACKNOWLEDGEMENTS

This report would not have been possible without the following people and organisations.

The National Lottery Heritage Fund have generously provided the resources to support this project and to produce this report. The original concept for the project was initiated by Jason Morden, Senior Conservation Officer at Nottinghamshire County Council. Jason had identified a gap in local knowledge regarding historic building conservation and drew up a brief with the architectural historian Clare Hartwell. Clare provided a solid research foundation with regard to the six villages she investigated. Also at Nottinghamshire County Council Janine Buckley and Steve Little provided sound advice and support throughout.

Helen Hay and David Fordham, authors of *New Coalfields, New Housing*, were expert and helpful with my early enquiries. Former miner and coalmining academic David Amos provided photographs, references, a wealth of knowledge and historical proof reading. Volunteers and visitors at Bilsthorpe Mining Museum were also insightful and hospitable.

Alison Davis at the University of the Nottingham School of Architecture helped with library membership, while the University of Nottingham library service loaned material during the difficult days of the Covid-19 pandemic. Similarly Nottinghamshire Archives remained open and expertly run during the lockdown restrictions of 2021. They helped with my many requests and cleared copyright. Picture Nottingham, Inspire Picture Archive, The Coal Authority and RIBA pix have also cleared copyright and provided quality high resolution images. Dan Lucas at Nottingham City Homes proof read a draft from a housing perspective. Dan also put me in touch with Brian Parbutt, who checked the document from someone growing up in Rainworth and Blidworth. My mum Julie Matthews kindly proof read the document. There are a number of Nottinghamshire coal miners within our family tree, such as my grandad Pete Matthews, who worked at Babbington Colliery, Cinderhill.

Every effort has been made to trace copyright holders and to obtain permission for the use of copyright material. The publisher apologises for any errors or omissions and would be grateful if notified of any corrections that should be incorporated in future reprints or editions of this book.

INDEX

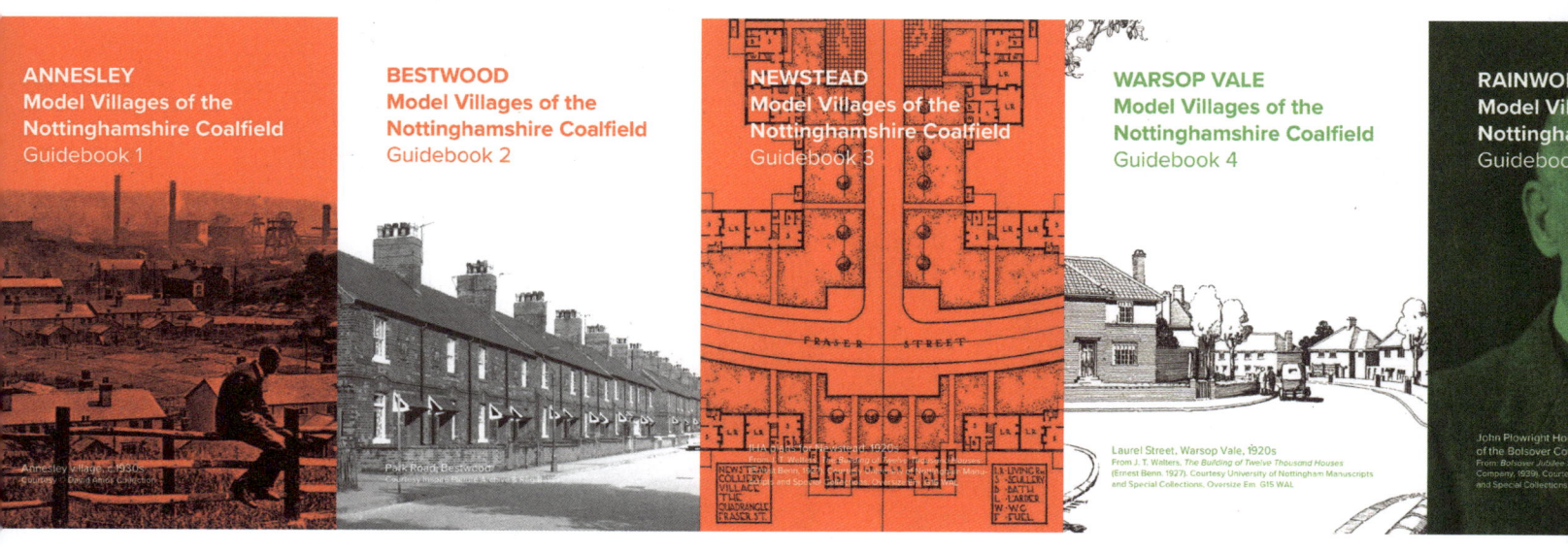

ANNESLEY
Model Villages of the Nottinghamshire Coalfield
Guidebook 1

Annesley Village, c.1930s
Courtesy © David Amos Collection

BESTWOOD
Model Villages of the Nottinghamshire Coalfield
Guidebook 2

Park Road, Bestwood
Courtesy Imperial Fields Archive & Reproduction

NEWSTEAD
Model Villages of the Nottinghamshire Coalfield
Guidebook 3

Newstead Village layout, 1920s
From J. T. Walters, *The Building of Twelve Thousand Houses* (Ernest Benn, 1927). Courtesy University of Nottingham Manuscripts and Special Collections. Oversize Em GIS WAL

WARSOP VALE
Model Villages of the Nottinghamshire Coalfield
Guidebook 4

Laurel Street, Warsop Vale, 1920s
From J. T. Walters, *The Building of Twelve Thousand Houses* (Ernest Benn, 1927). Courtesy University of Nottingham Manuscripts and Special Collections. Oversize Em GIS WAL

RAINWO
Model Vil
Nottingha
Guidebo

John Plowright Hou
of the Bolsover Coll
From *Bolsover Jubilee*
Company, 1920s. Courte
and Special Collections.

GUIDEBOOKS

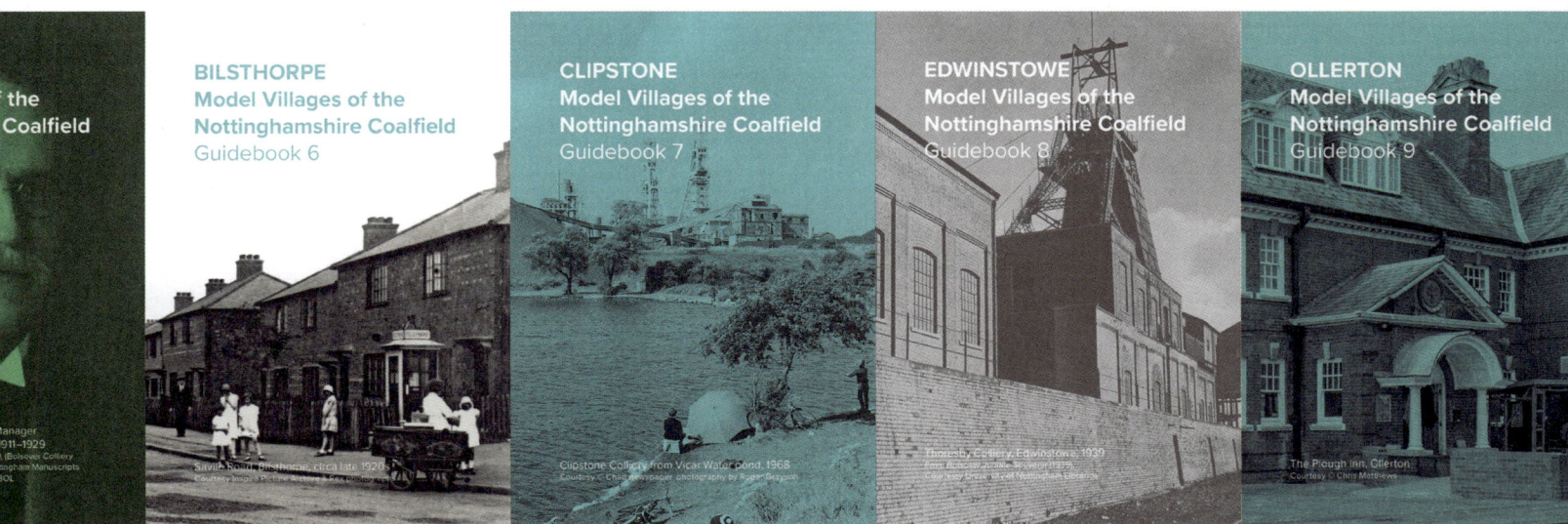

BILSTHORPE
Model Villages of the
Nottinghamshire Coalfield
Guidebook 6

CLIPSTONE
Model Villages of the
Nottinghamshire Coalfield
Guidebook 7

EDWINSTOWE
Model Villages of the
Nottinghamshire Coalfield
Guidebook 8

OLLERTON
Model Villages of the
Nottinghamshire Coalfield
Guidebook 9

To accompany the publication of this report a set of nine pocket-sized guidebooks have been produced, each of which covers a separate colliery village within the Nottinghamshire coalfield. The guides feature an historical introduction to the area, archive images, map and historic building illustrations.

This series is arranged thematically in accordance with the report: guides 1–3 cover the pioneer villages of Annesley, Bestwood and Newstead; guides 4 & 5 show the villages begun around the turn of century at Warsop Vale and Rainworth; and guides 6–9 give a detailed account of the achievements of the 1920s at Bilsthorpe, Clipstone, Edwinstowe and Ollerton.

Copies can be downloaded from the Miner2Major website
https://miner2major.nottinghamshire.gov.uk